LANGUAGE
FOR
MEANING

Language for Meaning

Level Yellow
Level Purple
Level Red
Level Blue
Level Orange
Level Green
Level Aqua
Level Brown

LANGUAGE FOR MEANING

CONSULTANT
Hugh Schoephoerster

Houghton Mifflin Company • **Boston**

Atlanta   Dallas   Geneva, Illinois
Hopewell, New Jersey   Palo Alto   Toronto

Grateful acknowledgment is given for the contributions of Paul McKee, M. Lucile Harrison, Margaret L. Hiatt, Annie M. McCowen, Anna M. Fagerlie, Arno J. Jewett, Robert W. Blake, Corinne Watson, Elwood L. Prestwood, and Mary Frances Floyd.

ACKNOWLEDGMENTS

"Central Park Tourney," by Mildred Weston. Reprinted by permission; © 1953 The New Yorker Magazine, Inc.

"City," by Langston Hughes. From *The Langston Hughes Reader*. Copyright © 1958 by Langston Hughes. Reprinted by permission of Harold Ober Associates, Incorporated.

"In the Fog," from *I Feel the Same Way*, by Lilian Moore. Text copyright © 1967 by Lilian Moore. Used by permission of Atheneum Publishers, Inc.

"Somersaults and Headstands," from *Stilts, Somersaults, and Headstands*, by Kathleen Fraser. Copyright © 1968 by Kathleen Fraser. Reprinted by permission of Atheneum Publishers, and Curtis Brown, Ltd.

PRINTED IN U.S.A.

ISBN: 0-395-25423-X

CONTENTS

5

UNIT 9   **Business Letters** • 274

DISCUSSIONS

When you talk, think about the people around you.
Who is listening to you? What things do all of you like?
These are the things to talk about. When people talk
about things they like, they enjoy themselves.

1 Talking with Others

To Read and Think Over

You are going to the zoo today! What animals will be there? Which animal is your favorite? Do you like the brightly colored birds in the Bird House? Do you like the long, lazy snakes in the Snake Pit? Or do you like the strong, graceful lions and leopards? Think about which animal is your favorite and what you can tell your classmates about it.

 ● Answer these questions in a sentence on your activity paper. Use the pictures for ideas.

1. What is the name of your favorite zoo animal?
2. What food does that animal eat?
3. Where is that animal's natural home? Does it live in the jungle or the desert?

Talking Together

A. Talk with your classmates about your favorite zoo animal. Use your paper for ideas. Tell interesting things you know about this animal.

B. Listen to your classmates talk about their favorite zoo animal. Try to learn something new about another animal.

Bird House

Follow these Guidelines when talking with others.

1. **Take part by telling or asking something.**
2. **Listen carefully to what others say.**
3. **Talk when no one else is talking.**

To Do By Yourself

Did you listen carefully to what your classmates said? Write three sentences that tell something you heard today about a zoo animal. Each sentence should tell something different about the animal.

2 Learning About Discussions

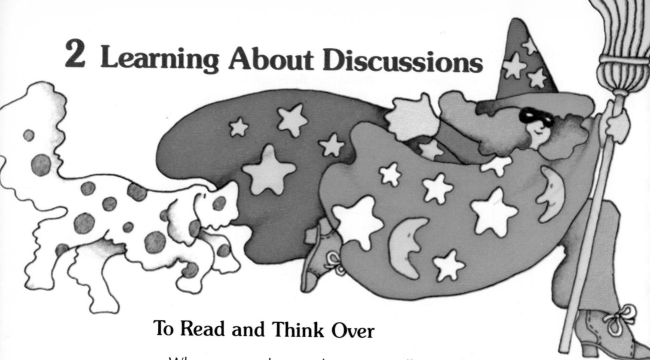

To Read and Think Over

When you and your classmates talk together about a problem or try to answer a question, you are having a **discussion**. Read this discussion about a Halloween party.

Odessa: It's almost Halloween. Let's make plans for a party.

Bert: That's a good idea. How about a costume...

Maureen: *(At the same time)* We should decide...

Bert: Oh, I'm sorry, Maureen. What were you saying?

Maureen: We should decide what kind of party to have. What were you starting to say, Bert?

Bert: I think we should have a costume party. Then we could all dress up.

Maureen: Oh, great! I'd like that. What about you, Odessa? Do you have some ideas for the party?

Odessa: I just want it to be fun.

Maureen: What do you mean by that? What would be fun?

Odessa: Maybe we could bob for apples.

● Decide if the sentence tells about something **Odessa, Maureen,** or **Bert** did. Complete each sentence with the name or names that fit best. Write each sentence on your activity paper.

1. _____ said what the subject of the discussion was.
2. _____ and _____ started to talk at the same time.
3. _____ stopped talking and let the other person speak.
4. _____ asked another person to explain something.
5. _____ gave an idea for a game.

Talking Together

A. Discuss with your classmates the sentences you wrote.

B. Did Maureen, Odessa, and Bert follow these GUIDELINES?

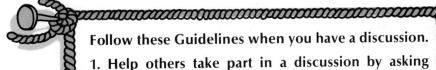

Follow these Guidelines when you have a discussion.

1. **Help others take part in a discussion by asking them to give their ideas.**
2. **If you do not understand what someone means, ask that person to explain.**
3. **If you and another person start to talk at the same time, one should let the other finish.**

To Do By Yourself

Think of three subjects you might discuss with your classmates. Write them on a sheet of paper.

3 Keeping to the Subject

To Read and Think Over

Maureen, Odessa, and Bert discussed the refreshments for the Halloween party. Did they keep to the subject?

Odessa: What are we going to do about refreshments?

Bert: Everyone can bring a favorite food to the party.

Odessa: Why don't you bring chocolate chip cookies, Maureen? The ones you make are delicious!

Maureen: Oh, but those aren't my favorite. You should taste my peanut butter cookies. I just made some for my grandfather's birthday.

Bert: Oh, that reminds me. My grandfather's birthday is next week. I've got to send him a card!

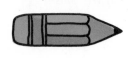 ● Write the answers to these questions on your activity paper.

1. What was the subject of the discussion?
2. Who did not keep to the subject of the discussion?
3. Which sentences were not about the subject? Write the sentences.

Talking Together

A. Discuss your answers with your classmates.

B. Why is it important to stay with one subject during a discussion? What happens if someone starts talking about something else?

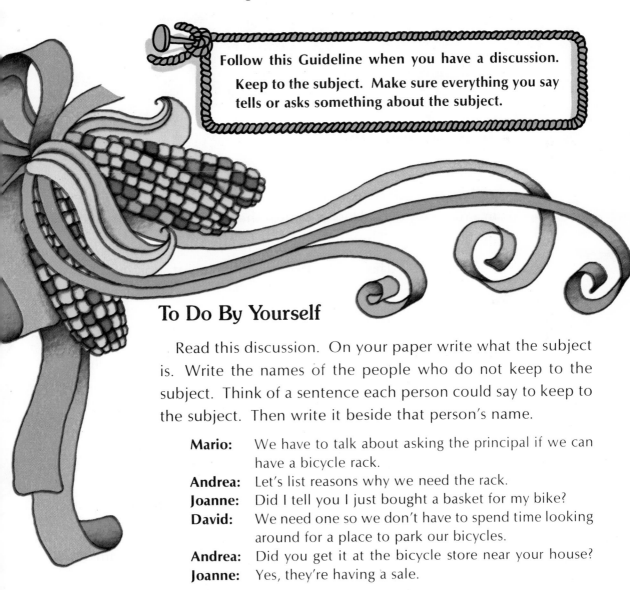

Follow this **Guideline** when you have a discussion.

Keep to the subject. Make sure everything you say tells or asks something about the subject.

To Do By Yourself

Read this discussion. On your paper write what the subject is. Write the names of the people who do not keep to the subject. Think of a sentence each person could say to keep to the subject. Then write it beside that person's name.

Mario: We have to talk about asking the principal if we can have a bicycle rack.

Andrea: Let's list reasons why we need the rack.

Joanne: Did I tell you I just bought a basket for my bike?

David: We need one so we don't have to spend time looking around for a place to park our bicycles.

Andrea: Did you get it at the bicycle store near your house?

Joanne: Yes, they're having a sale.

4 Finding Information

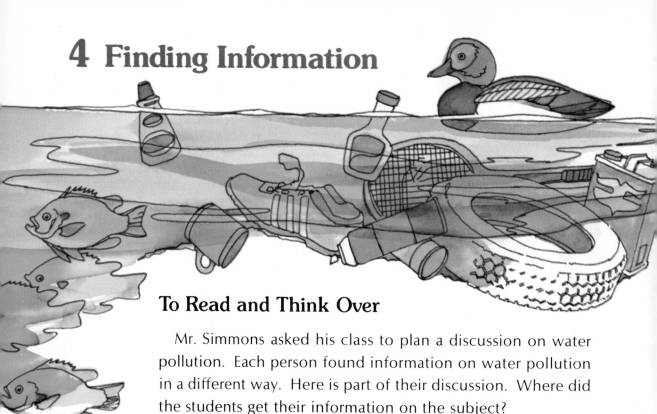

To Read and Think Over

Mr. Simmons asked his class to plan a discussion on water pollution. Each person found information on water pollution in a different way. Here is part of their discussion. Where did the students get their information on the subject?

Paula: This is a book on pollution I just took out of the library. It says that fish can't live any longer in some of our lakes and rivers.

Roger: That's right. My aunt Gloria is a scientist. She said polluted water can hurt wild ducks and geese.

Marion: I saw a TV program that showed how polluted water can be cleaned.

Clarence: Last summer my dad and I watched the polluted lake near our house being cleaned. The crew was there all summer. The lake really looks better.

If you are asked to plan a discussion, there are four ways to get information. You may read books and magazines about the subject of your discussion. You may see a TV program on the subject. You may listen to what other people say about it. Sometimes you see or do something that helps explain the subject.

 ● Finish these four sentences. Then write them on your activity paper.

1. Paula's information came from _____.
2. Roger's information came from _____.
3. Marion's information came from _____.
4. Clarence's information came from _____.

Talking Together

Talk about your answers with your classmates.

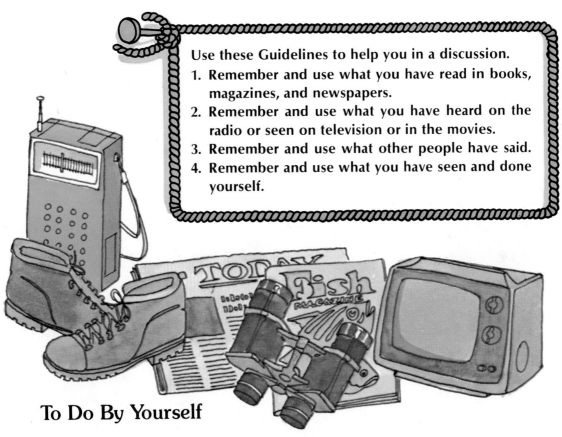

Use these Guidelines to help you in a discussion.
1. **Remember and use what you have read in books, magazines, and newspapers.**
2. **Remember and use what you have heard on the radio or seen on television or in the movies.**
3. **Remember and use what other people have said.**
4. **Remember and use what you have seen and done yourself.**

To Do By Yourself

Read these four questions. Write where you would look for information to answer each question.

1. What is first-class mail?
2. Who was Babe Ruth?
3. What is today's weather report?
4. What music is popular now?

5 Making Introductions

To Read and Think Over

Think of a time when you first met someone. Did you introduce yourself? Did someone else introduce you? Read the cartoons. They show some of the usual ways of introducing people.

● Copy this form on your activity paper. Pretend you are introducing a friend of yours to another friend. Fill in the names of your friends. Then say something interesting to help them start talking.

_____, this is my friend _____. _____ likes to

_____

so I thought you would like to meet her (him).

Talking Together

A. Share your introduction with your classmates. Listen to others read their introductions.

B. Discuss the cartoons.

Follow these Guidelines when someone new joins your group or when you join a new group.

1. Always introduce a new person to the group.
2. Try to say something interesting about the new person. This will help others begin a conversation with her or him.
3. Introduce yourself to a new person or group if no one knows you. Say your name and say something about yourself.

To Do By Yourself

Think of two people you might want to introduce to each other. Draw cartoons and show how you would introduce each one. Tell something interesting about each person so that they can begin talking together.

6 Using What You Have Learned

A. Think of a subject the whole class might like to discuss. For example, do you want to plan a class trip or program? Is there a question you want to discuss in social studies? Decide with your class which subject you would like most to discuss.

B. After you have chosen the subject for discussion, write the subject on a sheet of paper. Then write two things you can *tell* about the subject and two things you can *ask* about it. Discuss the subject with your classmates. Use your paper for ideas. Before you begin the discussion, review the GUIDELINES you learned on pages 13, 15, 17, and 19.

C. After the discussion, talk with the class about how well the class followed the GUIDELINES for discussion. Which GUIDELINES does the class need to follow more closely?

D. Think about the GUIDELINES you learned for making introductions on page 22. On your paper write how you would make these introductions:

    1. Introduce your sister Joanne to your friend Andy.
    2. Introduce your classmate Bob Taylor to your father.
       Use sentences like these to help you.
       _____, this is _____. _____, this is _____.

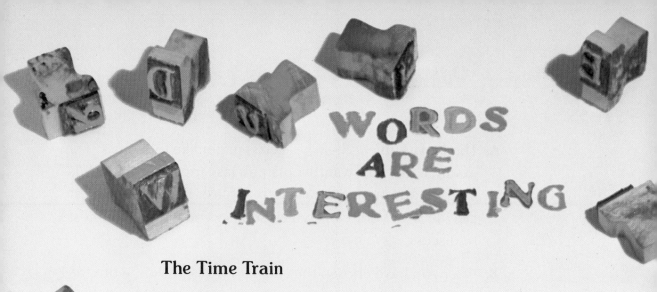

WORDS ARE INTERESTING

The Time Train

Suzi wrote a letter to her friend Sid about her ride on the Time Train.

Read Suzi's letter. Find the best synonym for each of the words in dark letters from the list of words with the same numeral. (Remember, synonyms are words that have almost, but not exactly, the same meaning.)

Copy the letter on your paper. Use the synonym in place of the word in dark letters.

Dear Sid,

There are some **different**[1] things to **say**[2] about our trip on the Time Train. First of all, it was **interesting**[3] to meet a **big**[4] dinosaur. The dinosaur seemed to enjoy **tasting**[5] the leaves.

Moving forward in time, we met some people building a temple. Next, the Time Train **paused**[6] in 1492. We watched Columbus **walk**[7] ashore in America.

Then some buttons on the Time Train were **crushed**[8]! So we are now **going**[9] into the future. Who knows when we will **join**[10] each other again?

Your friend,

Suzi

1	2	3	4	5
unusual	pronounce	exciting	healthy	drinking
changed	tell	important	firm	sipping
unlike	shout	easy	gigantic	eating

6	7	8	9	10
remained	step	damaged	traveling	meet
stopped	skip	destroyed	leaving	unite
rested	run	broken	running	gather

7 Using Your Voice Well

To Read and Think Over

Do you speak loudly enough to be heard? Do you speak slowly enough to be understood? Do you use your voice to make your meaning clear?

Look at the sentence printed here four times. Each time a different word is printed in dark type. Say the sentences to yourself. Each time say the word in dark type with more force than the other words. The words that you say with more force—with stress—make the meaning of the sentence clear.

1. **I** am going shopping with Sam.
2. I **am** going shopping with Sam.
3. I am going **shopping** with Sam.
4. I am going shopping with **Sam**.

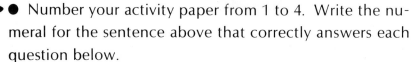

● Number your activity paper from 1 to 4. Write the numeral for the sentence above that correctly answers each question below.

1. Which sentence points out that *I am going, not Teresa?*
2. Which sentence points out that I am going *shopping, not ice-skating?*
3. Which sentence points out that *I am going for sure, not staying home?*
4. Which sentence points out that I am going *with Sam, not with Kenny?*

Talking Together

Discuss the answers you wrote with your classmates. Take turns reading the sentence "I am going shopping with Sam." Say a different word with force each time. Use your voice to make clear what the sentence means.

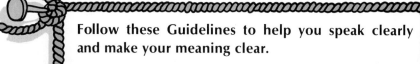

Follow these Guidelines to help you speak clearly and make your meaning clear.

1. Speak loudly enough to be heard.
2. Do not talk too fast or run your words together.
3. Speak with expression. The stress you put on certain words should help people understand your meaning.

To Do By Yourself

Look! It's snowing.

What word in these sentences would you stress to show you were happy it started to snow? Write the sentences on your paper and underline the word you would stress.

Write the sentences again. This time underline the word you would stress if you hadn't wanted snow.

8 Using Ate, Eaten; Gave, Given

To Read and Think Over

Read the sentences. The words **ate** and **eaten, gave** and **given** are used correctly. Can you tell why?

1. Who **has eaten** all the cookies?
2. They **were eaten** by mice!
3. I **ate** only one.
4. One **was given** to Rachel.
5. Rachel **gave** two cookies to Harriet.
6. **Were** any cookies **given** to you?

Notice that *eaten* and *given* are used with helping words. *Ate* and *gave* are never used with helping words.

● Copy these sentences on your activity paper. Choose the correct word.

1. Have you (ate, eaten) breakfast?
2. I (ate, eaten) breakfast an hour ago.
3. Has Andrea (ate, eaten) too?
4. Yes, she (ate, eaten) with me.
5. Breakfast is (ate, eaten) early here.
6. Who was (gave, given) the fruit?
7. We were (gave, given) some.
8. We had (gave, given) him some.
9. They (gave, given) her some apples.
10. Have we (gave, given) John any?

Talking Together

A. Discuss the sentences with your classmates. Did you use *ate, eaten, gave,* and *given* correctly?

B. Close your book and listen while your teacher reads these sentences. Listen to *ate, eaten, gave,* and *given* used correctly.

We have __1__ a big lunch.
First I __2__ two sandwiches.
Carol has __3__ two also.
Then three candy bars were __4__
By then I had __5__ too much.

Why was this __6__ to me?
I __7__ Eric a candy bar.
Has the last cookie been __8__ away yet?
I would have __9__ you some, but they have been __10__ away.

Follow these Guidelines when you use <u>ate</u>, <u>eaten</u>, or <u>gave</u>, <u>given</u>.

1. <u>Eaten</u> and <u>given</u> are used with helping words.
2. <u>Ate</u> and <u>gave</u> are never used with helping words.

To Do By Yourself

Copy on your paper the above sentences. In sentences 1 to 5 use *ate* or *eaten* correctly. In sentences 6 to 10 use *gave* or *given* correctly.

9 Using Did, Done; Saw, Seen

To Read and Think Over

Read the sentences. The words **did** and **done, saw** and **seen** are used correctly.

1. Mark **has seen** the fancy cake.
2. He **did** the shopping for it.

3. He **saw** Sharon frost the cake.
4. They **have done** all the decorating.

Did you notice that *done* and *seen* are always used with a helping word? *Did* and *saw* are never used with a helping word.

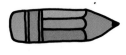

● Write these sentences on your activity paper. In sentences 1 to 5 use the correct word form, *did* or *done*. In sentences 6 to 10 use the correct word form, *saw* or *seen*.

1. Who has (did, done) the cleaning?
2. All of us have (did, done) it.
3. Jerry (did, done) the washing.
4. The sweeping was (did, done) by Sally and Donald.
5. They had (did, done) mopping too.
6. The colts (saw, seen) the barn.

7. A horse was (saw, seen) in the field.
8. Trudy had never (saw, seen) such a fast horse.
9. The horse (saw, seen) the apple in her hand.
10. We (saw, seen) the horse take the apple out of Trudy's hand.

Talking Together

A. Discuss the sentences with your classmates. Did you use *did, done, saw,* and *seen* correctly? If you did not understand how to use them correctly, ask your teacher for help.

B. Close your book and listen while your teacher reads these sentences. Listen to *did, done, saw,* and *seen* used correctly.

Has Andrew __1__ the work yet?
It is __2__ already.
Had he __3__ it in the morning?
Yes, it was __4__ before noon.
He and Peter had __5__ it together.

Have you __6__ Angela?
I __7__ her with Harriet.
Jacob __8__ them a few minutes ago.
They were __9__ in the playground.
Have they __10__ his father?

Follow these Guidelines when you use <u>did</u>, <u>done</u>, <u>saw</u>, and <u>seen</u>.
1. <u>Done</u> and <u>seen</u> are used with helping words.
2. <u>Did</u> and <u>saw</u> are never used with helping words.

To Do By Yourself

Copy on your paper the above sentences. In sentences 1 to 5, use *did* or *done* correctly. In sentences 6 to 10, use *saw* or *seen* correctly.

10 Using Came, Come; Ran, Run; Went, Gone

To Read and Think Over

Read these sentences. The words **came, come, ran, run, went,** and **gone** are used correctly. Which words are used with a helping word? Which words are not?

1. **Is** Larry **gone**?
2. He **went** to the movies with Neal.
3. They **came** here first.
4. They **had come** before lunch.
5. I **had run** downstairs to open the door.
6. Neal **ran** in.

Did you notice that *come, run,* and *gone* are used with a helping word. Did you notice that *came, ran,* and *went* are never used with a helping word?

● Read the sentences again. On your activity paper write in a column the numeral of each sentence that has a helping word. Then write the helping word and the word it helps beside the numeral.

Talking Together

A. Discuss your answers with your classmates. Did you choose the sentences that had helping words in them?

B. Close your book and listen while your teacher reads these sentences. Listen to *came, come, ran, run, went,* and *gone* used correctly.

Our cat, Button, has __1__ (ran, run) away.

We were not __2__ (went, gone) long.

When we __3__ (came, come) back, we didn't see her.

She was __4__ (went, gone).

But she had always __5__ (came, come) home for supper.

We have __6__ (ran, run) up and down the street, calling her.

Marlo __7__ (went, gone) around the block.

Look; she __8__ (ran, run) home with Button!

Button is __9__ (went, gone) again.

We __10__ (went, gone) too.

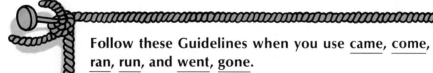

Follow these **Guidelines** when you use came, come, ran, run, and went, gone.
1. **Come, run,** and **gone** are used with helping words.
2. **Came, ran,** and **went** are never used with helping words.

To Do By Yourself

Copy the sentences above on your paper. Choose the correct word from the words in parentheses.

11 Using Is, Are; Was, Were

To Read and Think Over

You already know that **is, are, was,** and **were** can be used as helping words. These words can also be used alone.

Read the sentences. The words *is, are, was,* and *were* are used correctly. Which ones tell or ask about one person or thing? Which ones tell or ask about more than one?

1. Aunt Edie **is** here.
2. She **is** waiting for us.
3. Angelo **was** not ready.
4. We **were** ready on time.
5. Where **are** the twins?

Is, are, was, and *were* are special words. *Is* and *was* are used with one person or thing. *Are* and *were* are used with more than one person or thing.

The bird was in its nest.   **The birds were in their nest.**

● Copy these sentences on your activity paper. Choose the correct word.

1. The money (is, are) on the table.
2. (Is, Are) she ready to leave yet?
3. The shopping list (is, are) here.
4. (Is, Are) milk and bread on the list?
5. Yes, they (is, are).
6. My cousins (was, were) in a rowboat.

7. Muriel (was, were) planning to fish.
8. Joan and Ted (was, were) going swimming.
9. Suddenly a loud splash (was, were) heard.
10. The oars (was, were) floating away.

Talking Together

A. Discuss your sentences with your classmates. Did you use *is, are, was,* and *were* correctly?

35

B. Close your book and listen while your teacher reads these sentences. Listen to *is, are, was,* or *were* used correctly.

Who __1__ going to the circus?
We __2__ going.
__3__ John and Debbie going?
Debbie __4__ going to be there.
John __5__ not sure yet.
He __6__ at the circus last month.

His aunt and uncle __7__ there with him.
Their tickets __8__ for the last performance.
It __9__ sold out.
They __10__ glad they went.

Follow these **Guidelines** for using <u>is</u>, <u>are</u>, <u>was</u>, and <u>were</u>.
1. <u>Is</u> and <u>was</u> are used with <u>he</u>, <u>she</u>, <u>it</u>, and other words that name one person or thing.
2. <u>Are</u> and <u>were</u> are used with <u>we</u>, <u>you</u>, <u>they</u>, and other words that name more than one person or thing.

To Do By Yourself

Copy each sentence in section B. Use *is* and *are* in sentences 1 to 5. Use *was* and *were* in sentences 6 to 10.

12 Using What You Have Learned

A. Review the GUIDELINES you learned for the words in Lesson 8 to 11 on pages 29, 31, 33, and 36. Number a sheet of paper from 1 to 20. Next to each numeral write the correct word in place of the line with the same numeral.

Three cats __1__ (is, are) in the yard.

They __2__ (came, come) in over the fence.

They have __3__ (ate, eaten) all of Fuzzy's food.

When we __4__ (saw, seen) them there, they __5__ (ran, run) up a tree.

They were __6__ (gave, given) some milk.

They have all __7__ (came, come) down the tree except one.

The little orange kitten __8__ (went, gone) higher than the others.

He __9__ (is, are) on a branch.

He __10__ (was, were) crying before.

But now that he has __11__ (saw, seen) the milk, he has stopped.

He __12__ (is, are) trying to get down.

We have __13__ (did, done) everything we can to get him down.

But he has just __14__ (went, gone) higher up.

Kim __15__ (did, done) something brave.

She __16__ (was, were) scared too.

She __17__ (went, gone) up a tall ladder.

We __18__ (was, were) all watching her.

She __19__ (gave, given) the kitten milk.

Finally, she __20__ (came, come) down with the kitten.

B. Write ten sentences of your own. In each sentence use one of these words. Use a helping word such as *has, have, had, is, are, was,* or *were* in at least five of the sentences.

ate, eaten	gave, given
ran, run	is, are, was, were
went, gone	did, done
came, come	saw, seen

TRY IT AGAIN

Using Correct Word Forms (pages 28–36)

Copy each paragraph. Add the correct word form to each sentence.

A. Choose Ate or Eaten.

The campers __1__ a big breakfast this morning. It was one of the biggest they had ever __2__ . First, they __3__ pancakes. Then they __4__ sausages. When they had __5__ all the pancakes and sausages, they __6__ eggs and toast. The cook wondered if these campers had ever __7__ before.

Choose Gave or Given.

When will your class play be __8__ ? We have already __9__ it. We __10__ it last Friday. It was the best play the class has ever __11__ . The play will be __12__ again next week for our parents.

B. Choose the correct word in parentheses.

Has Juan (went, gone)[13] yet, Mrs. Perry? I (came, come)[14] as soon as I (did, done)[15] my work. I haven't (ran, run)[16] so fast in a long time.

Juan and Maria have (went, gone)[17]. They (did, done)[18] errands for me before they (went, gone)[19]. I haven't (saw, seen)[20] them since.

How long have they been (went, gone)[21]?

They have been (went, gone)[22] about a half hour. They said Jim had (ran, run)[23] right to the softball field. He (went, gone)[24] there an hour ago.

He promised the game wouldn't start until you (came, come)[25].

C. Copy the following paragraph. Use <u>Is</u> or <u>Are</u> in place of each space.

Where __1__ everyone? They __2__ going to the movies. __3__ the show good? There __4__ many people who liked it. __5__ you going again next week?

D. Copy the paragraph in section C again. This time use <u>Was</u> or <u>Were</u> in place of each space.

On Your Own

1. Look at the comic strip. It shows a problem. How would you solve that problem? Draw a picture or pictures and add conversation to solve the problem.

2. Billy has 100 different baseball cards. Paula has 75. Each has some baseball cards the other one would like to have. Draw a picture or pictures and add conversation that tells how they exchange cards.

3. One day you walked into your bedroom, and found your bed talking to the closet door. Read part of their conversation.

Closet door: I am tired of always being left open. Nobody ever closes me. If they do, they slam me.

Bed: Maybe nobody closes you, but at least you don't have people jumping on top of you all day.

What else do you think they will discuss? Write the rest of their conversation.

4. We don't always use words to give people information. Sometimes we use our hands. Sometimes the expression on our face tells a great deal. Look at these pictures. What information is being given? Draw pictures to show how you could give the following information without talking.

You are saying "no."
You are saying "yes."
You want someone to be quiet.

REPORTS

When you choose a subject for a report, choose something that interests you. What places have you read about in books? What things do you collect? What subject interests you?

Gather information on your subject and share it. Make your report exciting!

2

1 Choosing a Subject

To Read and Think Over

Everyone in Terry's and D.J.'s class has to write a report. D.J. and Terry are talking about how to choose a subject for a report. Read to see what they decide.

Terry: Have you thought of a subject yet?

D.J.: Our teacher said we should choose a subject we know well. I know about kites. I could write about the different kinds of paper used to make kites.

Terry: That doesn't sound very interesting. Why don't you write about the kite you made for the Fly-In Contest? Everyone wanted to know how you got the kite to look so much like a real bird.

D.J.: That's a great idea!

Now that D.J. has chosen a subject, he can write the title for his report.

 ● On your activity paper write the title you think would be most interesting for D.J.'s report.

My Kite	A Prize Kite
The Fly-In Contest	How to Fly a Kite
A Real Bird	How to Make a Prize Kite

Talking Together

A. Which title did you choose for D.J.'s report? Why?

B. Will D.J.'s classmates find the report interesting?

C. Why is it important to choose a subject that interests you?

Use these Guidelines when you choose a subject for a report.

1. **Choose a subject that interests you.**
2. **Choose a subject that will interest your classmates.**
3. **Choose a subject that you know well.**

Use this Guideline when you write a title.

> Begin the first word, the last word, and each important word in a title with a capital letter. In a title, words such as <u>a</u>, <u>an</u>, <u>by</u>, <u>from</u>, <u>for</u>, and <u>with</u> are not called important.

To Do By Yourself

Think of four subjects you might use for a report. Then think of an interesting title for each report. Write the titles on a sheet of paper. Be sure to write them correctly.

45

2 Keeping to the Subject

To Read and Think Over

You know that when you are taking part in a discussion, you should keep to the subject. The same is true when you make a report. Each sentence in your report should say something about the subject.

Read Juana's report. See if you can find three sentences that do not keep to the subject.

My Stamp Collection

When my parents get a letter with an interesting stamp, they give it to me. The first stamp in my collection came from Mexico. It was on a letter from my grandmother. My brother, Ramon, also has two coins from Mexico. My Aunt Rita went to Japan last summer and sent me two stamps. I also have stamps with inventors and other famous people on them. Ramon has a silver dollar. I keep my stamps in a special notebook. Ramon's coins are in a shoe box.

● Copy the sentences that do not belong in Juana's report on your activity paper.

Talking Together

A. Explain why each of the sentences you wrote on your activity paper does not belong in Juana's report.

B. Why do you think it is important to keep to the subject in a report?

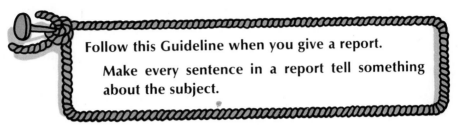

Follow this Guideline when you give a report.

Make every sentence in a report tell something about the subject.

To Do By Yourself

Terry decided to write a report called "My Favorite Zoo." Read the list of ideas Terry wrote. Some of the ideas belong in a report on this subject and some do not. On a sheet of paper write each idea that belongs in this report.

My Favorite Zoo

1. The name of the zoo
2. Where the zoo is
3. Other zoos I have visited
4. Kinds of animals at this zoo
5. What I like to do on Saturday afternoons
6. What I like to see first at the zoo

3 Telling Enough About the Subject

To Read and Think Over

When you give a report, it is important to choose a subject that you like. You also need to tell enough about the subject to make the report clear and interesting.

Read D.J.'s report to see if D.J. told enough about his prize kite.

A Prize Kite

I made a kite like a bird. I painted it. At the Fly-in Contest, my kite stayed in the air longer than any kite. I won first prize.

When D.J. finished giving his report, his classmates felt he had not given enough information about his prize kite. Here are some questions D.J.'s classmates asked.

What kind of bird did your kite look like?
Why did it stay in the air longer than any other kite?
When was the Fly-In Contest?

 ● On your activity paper write three other questions that D.J. should have answered in his report. Use words like **how, where,** and **who** to begin your questions.

Talking Together

A. Discuss the questions you wrote on your activity paper.

B. Look at the questions D.J.'s classmates asked and look at your questions. What are some of the words that can be used to begin questions?

Use this Guideline to help you make an interesting report.

Think of questions you would ask if you wanted someone to tell you about the subject. Use words like <u>who</u>, <u>what</u>, <u>where</u>, <u>when</u>, <u>why</u>, and <u>how</u> to begin your questions.
Use the answers in your report.

To Do By Yourself

Take the four titles you wrote for Lesson 1. Choose one of them. Write questions you would like answered about that subject. Use these questions to help you check your paper.

Do you know the answer to each question? If not, do you know where you can find the answer?
Did you begin each question with a capital letter?
Did you put a question mark at the end of each question?
Did you correct any errors you found?

4 Telling Things in the Right Order

To Read and Think Over

For a report to be interesting, you need to tell enough about the subject. You must also tell things in an order that makes sense. Look at the cartoon story. It does not make sense because the pictures are not in the right order.

● On your activity paper write the numerals of the cartoon in an order so that the cartoon tells a story.

Talking Together

A. Tell the cartoon story in the order it really happened.

B. Why is it important to tell things in the order in which they happened or were done?

C. Decide in what order the sentences should come in "How to Fool Your Friends." Use the numbers in talking about the sentences.

How to Fool Your Friends

1. First, pick out an old shirt and pants, a pair of mittens, and a pair of socks. **2.** When all the parts are stuffed, fasten them together with pins. **3.** Then stuff each piece of clothing with old newspapers. **4.** Blow up a large balloon for the head. **5.** Next, sit your dummy in a chair and give it a book to hold. **6.** Draw a face on the balloon and tie it to the shirt. **7.** Finally, invite your friends over to meet the new neighbor.

Follow this Guideline to help you write a report. Tell things in the order in which they happened or were done.

To Do By Yourself

On a sheet of paper write the sentences in the report "How to Fool Your Friends" in an order that makes sense. Do not copy the numerals on your paper.

5 Writing a Report

To Read and Think Over

You have been studying how to write a report. Read this finished report. What do you notice about the report?

A Pumpkin Snack

If you have an uncooked pumpkin, don't throw out the seeds. Roasted pumpkin seeds are good to eat for a snack. They are easy to make, too. Scoop out the seeds with a spoon. Separate them from the pulp and wash the seeds. Dry them and spread them out on a baking sheet. Then let them get crisp in the oven. After that, put a little salt on them and eat.

R. A. Lee

● Answer these questions on your activity paper.

1. Where is the writer's name?
2. Where is the title placed?
3. Where does the first word in the report begin?

Talking Together

A. Discuss the answers on your activity paper.

B. Look at the report again. Discuss with your classmates answers to these questions.

1. What is the subject?
2. Did R.A. keep to the subject? How do you know?
3. Did R.A. tell enough about the subject to make the report interesting? What did R.A. tell about it?
4. Did R.A. tell things in the right order? Explain your answer.

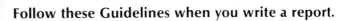

Follow these Guidelines when you write a report.

1. Write the title on a line by itself. Place it in the middle of the line. If you are not sure where to use capital letters in the title, look at page 45 again.
2. Skip a line. Indent the first line of the report. That means, begin it about five spaces farther to the right than the other lines.
3. Begin all the other lines even with one another. Keep equal margins on both sides.

To Do By Yourself

Choose a subject to write a report about from the list you made in Lesson 1. Think about the GUIDELINES you learned on pages 45, 47, 49 and 51 for writing a report. Now use them to write a report on the subject you chose. Follow the GUIDELINES in this lesson when you write your report.

6 Revising a Report

To Read and Think Over

When you write a report, you want it to be a good report. One way to be sure is to reread your report to see what needs to be changed. When you change words or sentences to improve your report, you are **revising** it. Revising is a necessary step in all writing.

After Kim Lee wrote her report, she read it again and decided to make some changes. This is the way she revised or changed her report.

Kim Lee

Saved from Drowning

1. Last Saturday Bob and I saw something exciting happen down at the river. **2.** A little boy fell from the bridge into the water. **3.** He was wearing a white shirt. **4.** Immediately, a woman rowed her boat toward the boy. **5.** Then the woman held out one of the oars to the boy. **6.** When the boy grabbed the oar, he was pulled toward the boat. **7.** The woman reached over and lifted the boy into the boat. **8.** We wondered if she would reach the boy in time.

54

 ● On your activity paper answer each of these questions.

1. Why did Kim take sentence 3 out of her report?
2. Why did Kim move sentence 8 to follow the new sentence 3?
3. Do you think Kim improved her report when she revised it? Why or why not?

Talking Together

A. Discuss the answers you wrote on your activity paper.

B. Why is it important to revise your work?

C. Read the GUIDELINES on page 56. Tell how they will help when you revise your work.

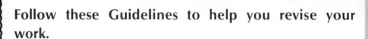

Follow these Guidelines to help you revise your work.

1. **Keep to the subject.**
2. **Choose a subject that interests others.**
3. **Tell enough about the subject.**
4. **Tell things in the order in which they happened.**
5. **Make each sentence say what you want it to say.**

To Do By Yourself

Revise the report you wrote for Lesson 5. If your report is hard to read after you have made all the changes, copy it on a clean sheet of paper.

7 Using What You Have Learned

A. You have written and revised your report. Now it is time to share your report with your classmates. Try to give your report without reading it. Be sure to speak so everyone in the class can hear you.

B. Listen politely to each person who gives a report. When the person is finished, ask questions about anything you did not understand.

C. Discuss the answers to these questions.

1. Which reports were the most interesting? Why?
2. Which speakers kept to the subject?
3. Which speakers told enough about their subjects?
4. Which speakers told about their subjects in an order that made sense?
5. Which speakers used their voices well?

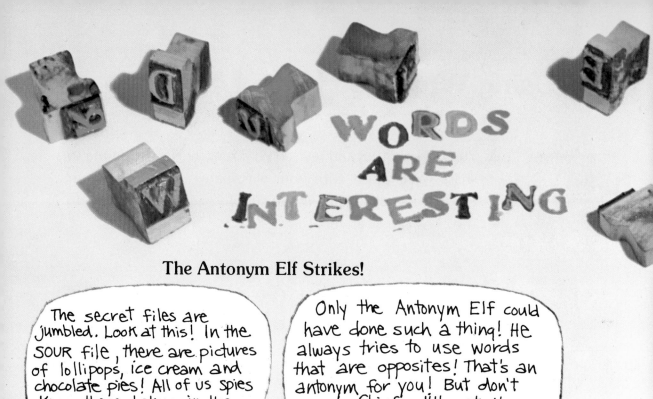

The Antonym Elf Strikes!

58

Show how you would put the files in order. Read the word in dark letters at the top of each list. You can see that words in dark letters do not describe the things named in that list!

Look in the Antonym Bank. Find the antonym, or opposite, of each word in dark letters. Write each antonym on your paper. Copy the list under each antonym.

1	2	3	4	5
heavy	**pale**	**fierce**	**swift**	**modern**
feathers	diamonds	cows	snails	dinosaurs
pins	gold	kittens	turtles	pyramids
papers	sun	puppies	inchworms	cavemen

6	7	8	9	10
weak	**still**	**dry**	**shallow**	**noisy**
steamshovels	swimming	water	caves	butterflies
cranes	skiing	rain	coal mines	clouds
tractors	mountain climbing	milk	oceans	thoughts

Antonym Bank

active	tame	light	ancient	powerful
silent	slow	deep	shiny	wet

8 What Is a Sentence?

To Read and Think Over

Which man is real? Which man is the model? The model has the same *form* as the man. It cannot move or do things the man can do. It only has the form of a man.

Any group of words that begins with a capital letter and ends with a punctuation mark has the *form* of a sentence. It looks exactly like a sentence, but it may just be a "model." A sentence tells or asks something by itself.

Each of these groups of words is a sentence.

> The man is standing in the window.
> Is he a real person?

Each of these groups of words has the *form* of a sentence but is not a sentence.

> This afternoon after school.
> The store on the corner?

● Look at these groups of words. On your activity paper write the groups of words that are sentences. Remember, a sentence is a group of words that tells or asks something by itself.

1. Marla hit the winning home run.
2. For Glenfield School.
3. Was the team proud of her?

4. The next game was canceled.
5. Because of rain.

Talking Together

A. Discuss the groups of words which you listed as sentences.

B. How can you decide if a group of words is a sentence?

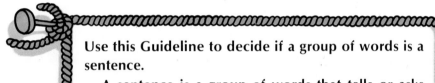

> **Use this Guideline to decide if a group of words is a sentence.**
>
> A sentence is a group of words that tells or asks something by itself. It starts with a capital letter and ends with a mark of punctuation.

To Do By Yourself

Rewrite this report. Make every group of words a sentence.

Lovable Wolves

Are wolves fierce animals? Who attack people? Many scientists say they are not. They say, instead, that wolves are kind and loving animals. Wolves live in families. With their children. Young wolves stay with their parents for a long time. Wolf families play together. And sing together at night.

9 Kinds of Sentences

To Read and Think Over

You know a group of words is a sentence when it tells or asks something by itself. There is more than one kind of sentence.

A sentence that is used to tell something is a **statement.** It ends with a period.

> Frankie's hat is yellow and red.

A sentence that is used to ask something is a **question.** It ends with a question mark.

> Is that Frankie's hat?

A sentence that is used to tell someone to do something is a **command.** It ends with a period.

> Give me Frankie's hat.
> Put on your hat, Frankie.

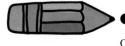 ● On your activity paper write three sentences of your own. One should be a *statement,* one a *question,* and one a *command.* Be sure to begin and end each correctly.

Talking Together

A. Read one sentence from your activity paper. Ask a classmate to tell what kind of sentence you wrote. If your classmate answers correctly, then that person should read a sentence from his or her paper.

B. Give a classmate a command about the picture on the next page. Your classmate should answer with either a statement or question.

Remember these Guidelines about sentences.

1. A statement is a sentence that tells something. It ends with a period.
2. A question is a sentence that asks something. It ends with a question mark.
3. A command is a sentence that asks or orders someone to do something. It ends with a period.

To Do By Yourself

Copy these sentences. Add the correct punctuation. Show what kind of sentence each is by writing *S* for statement, *Q* for question, and *C* for command.

1. Louella waited for us
2. What time did she get there
3. I'm not really sure
4. Try to remember, please
5. Was it before two o'clock
6. Where is Michael
7. He missed the bus
8. Find out when the next bus comes
9. Here comes Michael now
10. Hurry up; the game is ready to start

10 Sentences That Show Strong Feeling

To Read and Think Over

Sometimes a person uses a statement, question, or command in a way to show surprise, anger, or some other strong feeling. Suppose that on your birthday you were greatly surprised with a bicycle you did not expect to get.

The bicycle is beautiful!
How did you know I wanted one!
Let me take it outside and ride it!

Sentence 1 is a statement. Sentence 2 is a question. Sentence 3 is a command. Each is said with **strong feeling,** so each one is also an **exclamation.**

● On your activity paper write each of these sentences as an exclamation. Think about how you would say each one.

1. What are you doing
2. What I want is a cold drink
3. The paper cups are all gone
4. I'm weak from thirst

Talking Together

A. Try to read each sentence you wrote on your activity paper in a way that shows **strong feeling.** How did you end each sentence?

B. Help your classmates decide what punctuation mark should be used at the end of each of these sentences.

1. I'll take a box of peanuts, please
2. She hit a home run
3. I'm going to get a hot dog
4. What a good pitch that was
5. How could he have missed that easy catch

6. Hit it over the fence
7. Who did the team play yesterday
8. Did they win
9. They have won every game this season
10. What a catch that was

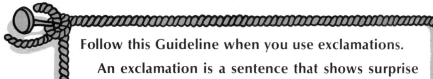

Follow this Guideline when you use exclamations.

An exclamation is a sentence that shows surprise or strong feeling. It ends with an exclamation mark.

To Do By Yourself

Copy the sentences in *Talking Together.* Add the punctuation mark you think should be used at the end of each sentence. Then write two sentences of your own that you might have used if you had been at the ball game.

11 Learning to Proofread

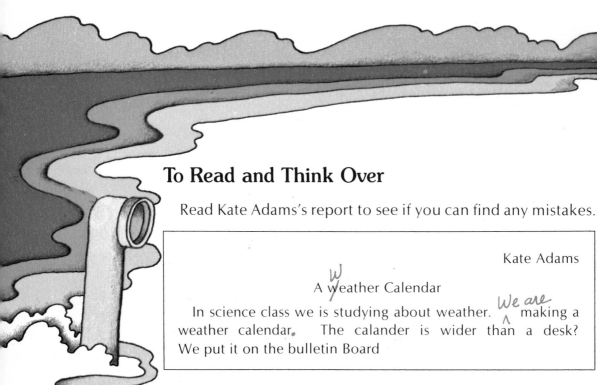

To Read and Think Over

Read Kate Adams's report to see if you can find any mistakes.

> Kate Adams
>
> A *w*eather Calendar
>
> In science class we is studying about weather. *We are* ^ making a weather calendar. The calander is wider than a desk? We put it on the bulletin Board

As Kate started to read over her report, she found some mistakes. She noticed in the title she had not begun *Weather* with a capital letter. She corrected that mistake. As she read on, she found a group of words that was not a sentence. She corrected that mistake, too. The work that Kate did in finding and correcting her mistakes is called **proofreading.**

● Help Kate finish proofreading her report. On your activity paper write the answers to these questions.

1. Which word is spelled wrong?
2. Which word is used incorrectly?
3. Which sentence has a mistake in punctuation?
4. Which word should not begin with a capital letter?

Talking Together

A. Discuss the way you corrected the mistakes in Kate's report.

B. Why is it important to proofread something you have written?

C. If your proofreading spoils the looks of your paper, what should you do?

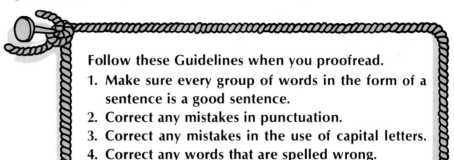

Follow these Guidelines when you proofread.
1. **Make sure every group of words in the form of a sentence is a good sentence.**
2. **Correct any mistakes in punctuation.**
3. **Correct any mistakes in the use of capital letters.**
4. **Correct any words that are spelled wrong.**
5. **Correct any words that are not used correctly.**

To Do By Yourself

Copy this report on a sheet of paper. Use the GUIDELINES in this lesson to correct any mistakes in sentences, punctuation, capital letters, or spelling. Proofread your paper to be sure it is written correctly.

The Starfish

Last summer I went to the seashore. Found a star fish. It is easy to recogonize a starfis because it looks like a star? Most star fish have five arms. some starfish have as many as Forty arms. What surprised me most about star fish is they are not really fish, but animals that lives in the see.

12 Using What You Have Learned

A. All of these groups of words have the form of a sentence. Some are sentences. Some are not. Copy each sentence on your paper.

1. Everyone on our block helped clean the vacant lot.
2. All day Saturday.
3. While I was raking.
4. I found a little box.
5. What was inside?
6. Everyone tried to guess.
7. Treasure in the box.
8. We tried to lift the box.
9. Too heavy.
10. In the box we found a heavy rock.

B. Here are some sentences you might hear people say at a Halloween party. The punctuation marks have been left out at the end of each sentence. Copy the sentences on your paper and add the correct punctuation marks.

1. Look at the ghost
2. Who is behind that mask
3. Would you like some candy
4. This is the best popcorn I ever had
5. My brother made my costume

6. Who is that in the rabbit costume
7. Step right up to duck for apples
8. I left my house at six o'clock to get here on time

C. Write two exclamations you might say at a Halloween party.

D. Proofread and correct any mistakes you find in this report. Copy the corrected report on your paper.

Hotball

Players sit in a circle and bat a soft Ball back and forth. The person who starts the game holds the ball for a second? then that person bats the ball so it bounces to someone else in the circle.

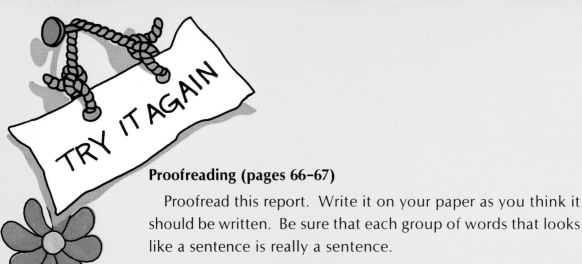

Proofreading (pages 66–67)

Proofread this report. Write it on your paper as you think it should be written. Be sure that each group of words that looks like a sentence is really a sentence.

Most fruits should not be picked before they are ripe. Except bananas, bananas that ripen on the plant will split open. Then insects get inside. And eat the fruit. Bananas must be picked while they are still green. Ripen best in a cool, dark place. When fully ripe. Yellow to the tips.

Kinds of Sentences (pages 62–65)

A. Read each group of words. If the group of words is a sentence, copy it on your paper.

1. Have you ever seen baby ducks?
2. Follow their mother.
3. The mother duck quacked.
4. Did the babies stay in line?
5. To the park?
6. They walked behind their mother.
7. The baby ducks swam in the pond.
8. Ate bread crumbs.
9. Care for her babies.
10. The mother duck watched the ducklings.

B. Copy each sentence. Add the correct end punctuation. Then show what kind of sentence each is by writing *S* for statement, *Q* for question, *C* for command, or *E* for exclamation.

1. What an awful storm that was
2. How the lightning flashed
3. Are you afraid of lightning
4. The clouds were an odd color
5. They were a greenish yellow
6. How dark the sky was before the storm
7. Weren't you surprised when it started to hail
8. What a noise the hail made on the roof
9. Look at the rainbow
10. This is the first rainbow I have ever seen

DO YOU REMEMBER ?

Using Correct Words Forms (pages 28-36)

Copy each sentence. Choose the correct word from the ones in parentheses.

1. (Is, Are) you going with the class?
2. Two buses had (came, come) to get us.
3. We had (saw, seen) them waiting.
4. Sam and Anna (did, done) a strange thing.
5. They haven't (ate, eaten) their lunch.
6. The teacher (went, gone) with us.
7. A guide (gave, given) us a map.
8. Lew has (ran, run) to the shark pool.
9. Six little sharks (was, were) there.
10. The children (was, were) not afraid.
11. A glass wall (was, were) around the sharks.
12. (Was, Were) the seal funny?
13. Warren (was, were) nowhere to be found.
14. Bert and I thought we had (saw, seen) him.
15. Finally Bert (saw, seen) him.
16. He (went, gone) to the cafeteria.
17. Warren had (ate, eaten) a hamburger.
18. We had (went, gone) to the pool to look for him.
19. We (was, were) afraid that a shark ate him.
20. We all (ran, run) back to our teacher.

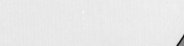

Sentences (pages 60–61)

Write the word groups that are sentences on your paper.

1. The next day.
2. We will have a picnic.
3. Because of rain?
4. Will you go with us tomorrow?
5. We can play softball.

Kinds of Sentences (pages 62–65)

Write the sentences below. Begin and end each one correctly.

1. where is George hiding
2. he likes this game
3. someone saw him in the closet
4. do you think he's under the chair
5. that cat is really a lot of fun

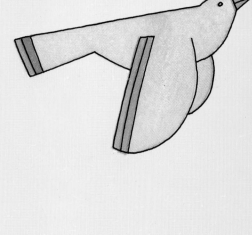

On Your Own

1. Write a report about one of the "Why I Like" subjects. Remember to tell all the interesting facts. If you do not wish to write about any of these titles, you may write a "Why I Like" report about something else.

   Why I Like Holidays
   Why I Like Sports
   Why I Like TV

2. Look at the pictures of all the hands. Choose one pair of hands. To whom do they belong? Write a story about that person and what the person does with his or her hands.

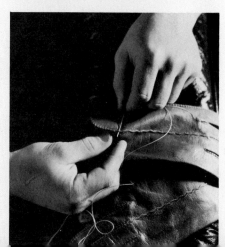

3. Read these two sentences.

> The sand felt as hot as burning coals.
> My hands were as cold as two frozen snowballs.

Here are the beginnings of five sentences. Add words to each one to make an interesting sentence.

> The ride was as bumpy as . . .
> The bell was as loud as . . .
> The baby was as funny as . . .
> I am as hungry as . . .
> The woman is as tall as . . .

4. You have heard or read about astronauts orbiting in space. Pretend that you had a chance to ride in a space capsule. How would it feel as you left earth? Who would you take with you? Where would you go? What would you find there? What might you bring back to earth? Write a report about your make-believe ride in space.

LISTENING

Sounds and voices are all around you. Some are important to you and some are not. When you tune in to a special voice or sound, you are listening. Learn to be a good listener. You will learn more things and enjoy more things.

1 Taking a Telephone Message

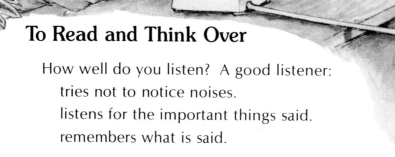

To Read and Think Over

How well do you listen? A good listener:
  tries not to notice noises.
  listens for the important things said.
  remembers what is said.

Are you a good listener? Let's find out.

Your teacher will pretend to be someone calling on the telephone. Listen carefully. You will need to tell someone else what your teacher said. You will need to remember the important facts.

NOW LOOK UP . . . AND LISTEN.

● Did you remember the important facts in the telephone call? Pretend the following sentences are part of the message for your mother. Complete the message by filling in the spaces. Write the message on your activity paper.

_____ called you. She said _____. She would like you to _____.

Talking Together

A. Discuss the message you wrote on your paper.

B. What problems did you have in listening to your teacher? Were you bothered by noises? Were you able to keep your mind on what your teacher was saying?

Follow these Guidelines to be a good listener.

1. **Listen to what is being said.**
2. **Listen for the important facts.**
3. **Be able to tell what the speaker said in your own words.**

To Do By Yourself

Pretend you took a telephone message for your friend. Complete the message by adding your own words. Write the complete message on your paper.

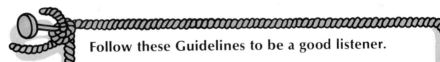

This is _____. I was supposed to meet _____ at _____ o'clock in front of _____. We were going to go to _____. But I can't go because _____.

Work with another pupil. Take turns listening to each other's message. Check each other's paper for the correct message.

2 Listening for the Main Idea

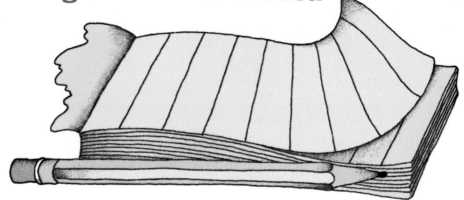

To Read and Think Over

When you gave your mother the telephone message from Pat Adams, did you include everything Pat said? Probably you only needed to listen and give your mother the main points.

Here is a different listening activity. Listen as your teacher reads a brief story. Think about the **main idea** of the story.

NOW LOOK UP . . . AND LISTEN.

● The title of a selection often tells you the main idea of the selection. Study the following titles. On your activity paper write the title that best states the main idea of the selection you heard.

    1. How Fire Helped People of Long Ago
    2. How the Milky Way Came to Be
    3. The Girl Who Played with Fire

Talking Together

A. Which title did you pick as the main idea of the selection your teacher read? Give reasons for your choice. Did your classmates pick the same one?

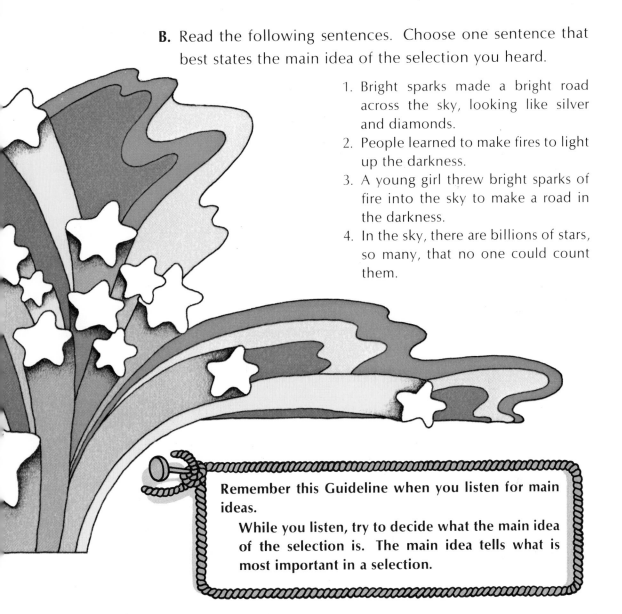

B. Read the following sentences. Choose one sentence that best states the main idea of the selection you heard.

1. Bright sparks made a bright road across the sky, looking like silver and diamonds.
2. People learned to make fires to light up the darkness.
3. A young girl threw bright sparks of fire into the sky to make a road in the darkness.
4. In the sky, there are billions of stars, so many, that no one could count them.

Remember this Guideline when you listen for main ideas.

While you listen, try to decide what the main idea of the selection is. The main idea tells what is most important in a selection.

To Do By Yourself

Try writing your own summary of the story you heard at the beginning of this lesson. You have already identified a title for the selection. Now, write three sentences on your paper that tell the story.

3 Words in Advertising

To Read and Think Over

Suppose these pictures were on your TV set! Look at the pictures. Your teacher will read what the announcer would say. Listen carefully for words that tell you how the soap makes you feel.

NOW LOOK UP . . . AND LISTEN.

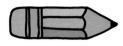 ● On your activity paper make a list of any words the announcer used that tell how you might like to feel.

Talking Together

A. Share your list of words with your classmates. Which words should you add to or take off your list?

B. What feeling does each word in your list suggest? What picture does it bring to your mind? Do the words in your list suggest pleasant feelings? Why or why not?

C. Do you think you might like to use this soap? Why?

Use these Guidelines when you listen to an ad.

1. **Listen for facts in an ad. Facts should help you decide whether or not to buy a product.**
2. **Some words in an ad make you feel good. These words should not help you to decide whether or not to buy a product.**

To Do By Yourself

Study the following lists of words. Make a list of products that might use words like these in an ad.

dazzling	creamy	grease-cutting
brilliant	buttery	fast-acting
snow-white	mouth-watering	grime-chasing
spotless	tempting	dirt-fighting

4 Listening for Facts and Opinions

To Read and Think Over

When you listen to people talk, it is often important to know whether they are stating a **fact** or giving an **opinion.**

When you give an opinion, you are saying *what you think.* Some people may think the same as you do. Others may not.

When you state a fact, you are talking about something *you can prove.* A fact is either true or not true.

Look at the picture. Which person stated a fact? Which person stated an opinion?

● Number your activity paper from 1 to 10. Listen as your teacher reads ten sentences. After you hear each statement, write *F* if it is a statement of fact. Write *O* if it is a statement of opinion.

Talking Together

A. Share the answers on your activity paper with your classmates. Which statements were opinions? Which ones were facts? If you and your classmates did not agree on which statements were facts and which were opinions, ask your teacher to read the statements again.

B. Would a statement which began *I think* be a statement of fact or opinion? Why?

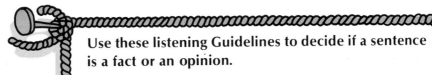

Use these listening Guidelines to decide if a sentence is a fact or an opinion.

1. **An opinion tells what someone thinks. It often contains words like <u>I think</u>.**
2. **A fact can be true or false. It does not contain words like <u>I think</u>.**

To Do By Yourself

On your paper, write *Fact* for each sentence below that is a fact. Write *Opinion* for each one that is an opinion.

1. There are nine players on a baseball team.
2. I feel baseball is harder to play than football.
3. The first crossword puzzle was made up in England.
4. I think crossword puzzles are fun to do.
5. I feel that Russia is too cold a place to visit in the winter.
6. The temperature was zero yesterday.
7. I think it was cold.

85

5 Using What You Have Learned

A. Choose a partner and act out these telephone conversations.

1. Mrs. Rothwell, your mother's friend, telephones. Your mother is at a neighbor's house. Mrs. Rothwell wants to borrow your mother's drill. She needs it right away.

   Talk to Mrs. Rothwell; then call your mother and give the message to her.

2. Your grandfather calls. You are the only one at home. He is expecting all of you for dinner on Friday at 6:00. He won't have time to go to the bakery and would like you to bring dessert.

   Talk to your grandfather, and then give the message to your mother or father.

Discuss with your classmates how well you gave each message. Did you understand the main idea of what was being said? Did you know what was important and remember to tell it?

B. Pick one of these products: soap, a soft drink, cereal, or a toy. Write an advertisement for it. Use words that will make the listener feel good or happy. Ask your classmates to listen for (1) words which describe how the product is supposed to make the listener feel; (2) words which describe what the product is or what it does.

C. Look at some advertisements in magazines.
Find five statements in them that are facts.
Find five statements which are opinions.

D. Listen carefully to a selection which your teacher will read to you. When your teacher has finished reading, choose, from the titles listed, the best title for the selection. To choose the best title, think about the main idea in the selection your teacher read.

1. Bees Can Dance
2. Bees Have a Special Way of Communicating
3. How Bees Get Food to the Hive

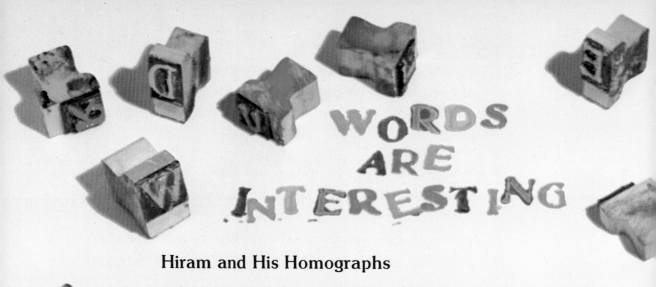

WORDS ARE INTERESTING

Hiram and His Homographs

Hiram loves stories. Sometimes, though, he reads sentences that bring strange pictures to his mind. For example, Hiram read these sentences in one of his books.

The guests toasted the bride and groom.
The singer was surrounded by her fans.
We found some bats sleeping in the attic.

Hiram's problem is that he does not know about **homographs.** Homographs are words that have the same spelling but different meanings. Some homographs also may sound different when you say them aloud.

Please wind the clock.
Listen to that wind!

How can Hiram solve his problem with homographs? Here are two ways:

1. He can study the sentence, or context, in which the word appears. It may give him a clue to the word's meaning. From the context, do you know what *toasted, fans,* and *bats* mean in the sentences on page 88?

2. Hiram can use the dictionary. Each homograph and its meaning is listed in the dictionary. Hiram must try out these meanings until he finds one that fits the sentence.

Now you try it. Use the context and the dictionary to find the meanings of the words in dark letters. Write the meaning of each homograph in your own words.

1. Nina caught a **skate** while she was fishing.
2. Elmo made a **racket** all night.
3. A huge golden **coach** rolled through the streets.
4. Martha put a **seal** on her letter.
5. I saw a **tear** on his cheek.
6. Robin Hood could use a **bow** well.
7. Frank sat on the **bank** of the river.
8. The guests danced at the **ball.**
9. The captain was afraid the ship would **sink.**
10. They will **bear** the blame for their actions.

89

6 Learning About Nouns

To Read and Think Over

Look at the following sentences.

1. A boy ran through the gate.
2. The poodle was quiet.

The words in color in each sentence are **nouns.** A **noun** can be the name of a person, the name of a place, or the name of an object or thing. Look at the words that come before the nouns in these sentences.

The girl is eating **an** apple.
A dog was running down **the** street.

Did you notice the words that come before each word in color? **The, a,** and **an** are special words. They are called **determiners.** A determiner tells you that a noun will soon follow in the sentence. A determiner is a noun signal.

Here are some other determiners:

this   that   these   those

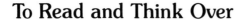 ● In these sentences the determiners are in dark letters. After each determiner there is a space for a noun. Add a noun to complete each sentence. Look around the classroom to help you decide on words to use. Then copy each sentence on your activity paper.

1. I can see **a** _____.
2. **This** _____ is on **the** _____.
3. **That** _____ is near **the** _____.
4. I can see **those** _____.
5. I often use **these** _____.

6. Lend me **a** _____.
7. **This** _____ is here.
8. **A** _____ rang.
9. **The** _____ is here.
10. **A** _____ fell down.

Talking Together

A. Discuss the sentences you wrote.

B. What is a noun? If you are not sure a word is a noun, place it in this frame: I like the _____. If the word fits in the frame, it is a noun.

C. Name some determiners. What kind of word usually follows a determiner?

Use these Guidelines to find nouns.

1. **A word is a noun when it is used to name a person, place, or thing.**
2. **A noun can fit into a sentence frame like this one. I like the _____.**
3. **Words like <u>the</u>, <u>a</u>, <u>this</u>, and <u>those</u> are called determiners. They are usually followed by nouns.**

To Do By Yourself

Copy these sentences on your paper. Circle each determiner. Underline each noun.

1. That girl saw the basket.
2. The snakes lay inside.
3. "Are those snakes dangerous?" someone asked.
4. "When I play this flute, the snakes will start to dance," said the owner.
5. The girl watched as a snake began to move.

7 Forming Plural Nouns

A BOX

SOME BOXES

To Read and Think Over

You know that a noun is the name of a person, a place, or a thing. A noun that names one thing is called a **singular** noun. A noun that names more than one thing is called a **plural** noun.

Look at these pairs of words. The top word is singular. The bottom word is plural. Study these words carefully. Notice how each plural is formed. What letters are added? What letters are changed?

cat	box	knife	baby	dish
cats	boxes	knives	babies	dishes

 ● Answer these questions on your activity paper.

1. Which word forms the plural by adding **-s?**
2. Which two words form the plural by adding **-es?**
3. Which word forms the plural by changing **-f** to **-v** and adding **-es?**
4. Which word forms the plural by changing **-y** to **-i** and adding **-es?**

Talking Together

A. Share the answers you wrote on your paper with your classmates.

B. Think of a singular noun. Call on a classmate to name the plural form and spell the word. Then ask that person to name another singular noun and call on someone else to spell the plural form.

Use these Guidelines when writing the plural forms of nouns.

1. Most nouns form their plurals by adding -s to the singular.

   tree   trees   street   streets

2. Nouns that end in -s, -ch, -sh, or -x form their plurals by adding -es.

   lunch   lunches   dish   dishes

3. Most nouns that end in -f or -fe form their plurals by changing the -f or -fe to -v and adding -es.

   wolf   wolves   wife   wives

4. Many nouns that end in -y form their plurals by changing -y to -i and adding -es.

   puppy   puppies

   Some nouns, however, just add -s.

   day   days

To Do By Yourself

Write the plural form for each noun. Then write a sentence using each plural form.

1. bench	3. lake	5. ruby	7. glove	9. boat	11. fly
2. kiss	4. key	6. calf	8. wish	10. loaf	12. tax

8 More Plural Nouns

ONE DEER   TWO DEER

To Read and Think Over

Most plurals are formed by adding -s or -es to a noun. Not all plurals are formed this way. Some nouns form their plurals in other ways. Study these words. In each of these words, a letter or letters in the middle of the word are changed to form the plural.

tooth — teeth   mouse — mice
foot — feet   woman — women
goose — geese   man — men

Now look at these words. The singular and plural forms are the same.

sheep — sheep
deer — deer
moose — moose

These words add letters at the end to form the plural.

child—children   ox—oxen

94

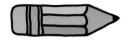

● On your activity paper copy these singular nouns. Then write the plural form next to each one.

1. tooth   6. goose
2. deer   7. woman
3. man   8. mouse
4. child   9. ox
5. sheep   10. moose

Talking Together

A. Look at each pair of words you wrote. What letter or letters in the plural form are different from the singular form?

B. Look at this list of singular nouns. If you are asked to do so, give the plural form of each singular noun.

1. map   6. self
2. zero   7. man
3. army   8. fish
4. foot   9. zoo
5. church   10. family

Use these Guidelines to write the plural forms of some nouns.

1. **Some nouns change a letter or letters in their spelling to form the plural.**

    woman — women   mouse — mice

    child — children   tooth — teeth

2. **Some nouns have the same form in the singular and the plural.**

    deer — deer   sheep — sheep

To Do By Yourself

Rewrite this story. Change each underlined noun from the singular form to the plural form.

The goose, mouse, and the sheep were walking in the woods. The moose saw them and called for help. "The deer fell into a trap," they explained. They examined the cut foot and broken tooth of the deer. Then they sent the sheep to get help. "And please hurry," they said. "Don't stop to play with the child or the fish."

9 Possessive Nouns

my friends' pets

To Read and Think Over

Look at these groups of words. Study the words in color.

my **mother's** car   my **brothers'** gloves
my **father's** book   my **sisters'** boots
the **dog's** dish   my **friends'** pets

You know that words like **mother** and **brothers** are nouns. So are **mother's** and **brothers'.** They are special forms of nouns called **possessive nouns.**

my mother's car   the car that belongs to my mother
my brothers' gloves   the gloves that belong to my brothers

Study the examples again. Notice how the apostrophe is used. When the possessive noun is singular, the apostrophe comes before the *s*. When the possessive noun is plural, the apostrophe comes after the *s*.

 ● On your activity paper rewrite each of these groups of words, using the possessive form of the noun. The first one has been done for you.

Remember! For the singular form of the noun, add 's. For the plural form of the noun, add s'.

1. the bed that belongs to the cat   <u>the cat's bed</u>
2. the nests that belong to the birds   _____
3. the shoes that belong to Alice   _____

Talking Together

A. Discuss the answers you wrote on your activity paper.

B. Say *friends, friend's,* and *friends'* aloud. Do they all sound alike? Are they written in the same way?

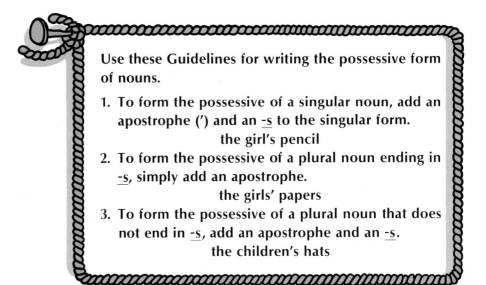

Use these Guidelines for writing the possessive form of nouns.

1. **To form the possessive of a singular noun, add an apostrophe (') and an -s to the singular form.**
   the girl's pencil
2. **To form the possessive of a plural noun ending in -s, simply add an apostrophe.**
   the girls' papers
3. **To form the possessive of a plural noun that does not end in -s, add an apostrophe and an -s.**
   the children's hats

To Do By Yourself

A. Write a sentence using each of these possessives.

1. aunt's	3. wolves'	5. mouse's	7. players'	9. puppy's
2. men's	4. deer's	6. children's	8. friends'	10. ladies'

10 Proper and Common Nouns

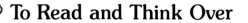

To Read and Think Over

Compare these pairs of sentences.

I like my **sister.**   I like Roberta.
Sue lives in a **city.**   Sue lives in Detroit.
My friend eats **candy.**   My friend eats Sugarettes.

Each word in boldface type is a **common noun.** *Sister* is a person. *City* is a place. *Candy* is a thing. A common noun names any person, place, or thing.

Each word in color is a **proper noun** because each names a particular person, place, or thing. *Roberta* is a particular person. *Detroit* is a particular place. *Sugarettes* is a particular thing. A noun that names a particular person, place, or thing is a proper noun.

● Divide your activity paper into two columns. Study these nouns. Write all the common nouns in one column. Write all the proper nouns in the other column.

Montreal	orange	Montana	Chicago
hotel	Crunchy Oats	Elm Street	dog food
pencil	David	notebook	June
Atlantic Ocean	friend	Easter	Friday

Talking Together

A. Discuss the lists you wrote with your classmates. How does a proper noun always begin?

B. For each common noun, give a proper noun. Remember that a proper noun is the name of a particular person, place, or thing.

man	boy	country	cookie
woman	city	river	toothpaste
girl	state	soft drink	car

Use these Guidelines for recognizing and writing proper nouns.

1. **A proper noun names a particular person, place, or thing.**
2. **A proper noun can be more than one word.**
3. **A proper noun begins with a capital letter.**

To Do By Yourself

Some of the words below should have capital letters because they are proper nouns. Find the proper nouns and write them on your paper. Remember to begin each proper noun with a capital letter.

1. market street
2. valley
3. foster school
4. street
5. springtime soap
6. school
7. edith flynn
8. mohawk valley
9. soap
10. doctor

11 Using What You Have Learned

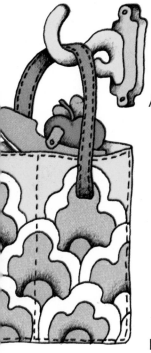

A. Write five sentences. Begin each sentence with a determiner from the list on the left and a noun from the list on the right.

DETERMINERS	NOUNS
the	bag
a	map
an	muffin
this	shoe
that	apple

B. Rewrite each sentence. Write the plural form of the word in parentheses in place of the line.

1. We are going to three (party) _____ on Halloween.
2. The meadow was filled with wild (grass) _____.
3. The (leaf) _____ were a pale green color.
4. In the brook, three (fish) _____ swam by.
5. Pick up your (foot) _____ while I sweep.

C. Write a proper noun for each of the following common nouns.

1. a month
2. a city
3. a holiday
4. a building
5. a club
6. a book
7. a day
8. a street
9. a country
10. a river
11. a kind of car
12. a kind of cereal
13. a pet
14. a friend
15. an ocean
16. a state
17. a doctor
18. a school
19. a park
20. a province

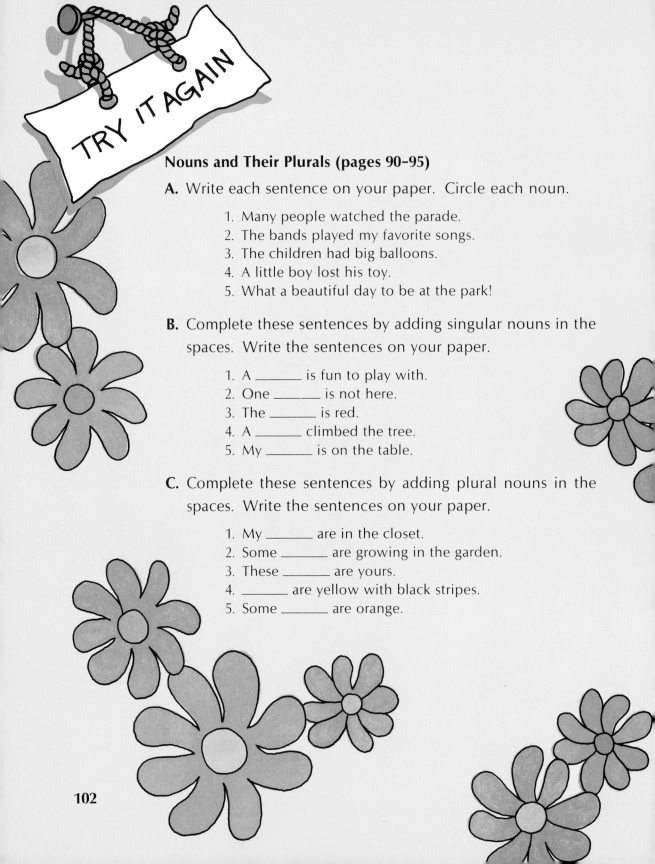

Nouns and Their Plurals (pages 90–95)

A. Write each sentence on your paper. Circle each noun.

1. Many people watched the parade.
2. The bands played my favorite songs.
3. The children had big balloons.
4. A little boy lost his toy.
5. What a beautiful day to be at the park!

B. Complete these sentences by adding singular nouns in the spaces. Write the sentences on your paper.

1. A _____ is fun to play with.
2. One _____ is not here.
3. The _____ is red.
4. A _____ climbed the tree.
5. My _____ is on the table.

C. Complete these sentences by adding plural nouns in the spaces. Write the sentences on your paper.

1. My _____ are in the closet.
2. Some _____ are growing in the garden.
3. These _____ are yours.
4. _____ are yellow with black stripes.
5. Some _____ are orange.

Possessive Nouns (pages 97–98)

Write each sentence. Add the correct possessive form from the words in parentheses.

1. What is that (girl's, girls') name?
2. Where is the (puppy's, puppies') toy?
3. All the (teacher's, teachers') coats are in the gym.
4. Have the (pilot's, pilots') caps been found?
5. Three (boy's, boys') uniforms are too small.

Common and Proper Nouns (pages 99–100)

Write a proper noun for each of these common nouns.

1. a teacher
2. a road
3. a town
4. a dog
5. a newspaper

DO YOU REMEMBER ?

Kinds of Sentences (pages 62–65)

Copy each sentence. Begin and end them all correctly. Put *S* after each statement and *Q* after each question. Put *C* after each command and *E* after each exclamation.

1. is Vito going to the movies
2. the show is about a lost island
3. people land there on a raft
4. what happens to them
5. do they see a lot of dinosaurs
6. dinosaurs are everywhere
7. stay away from them
8. what a strange island
9. what friendly dinosaurs
10. did Vito like the movie

Using Words Correctly (pages 28–33)

Copy each sentence. In place of the space, use the correct word from the words in parentheses.

1. (ate, eaten)   Mike has _____ already.
2. (ran, run)   Yesterday she _____ too fast.
3. (went, gone)   Has your sister _____ to work?
4. (did, done)   They _____ their work quietly.
5. (came, come)   Had the mail _____ on time?
6. (saw, seen)   Last night they _____ a comet.

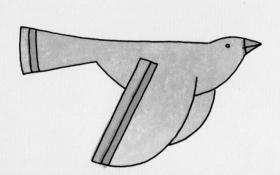

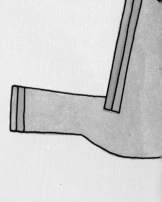

Proofreading (pages 66-67)

Proofread this report. Write it on your paper as you think it should be written.

The Big Dipper

The seven stars in the Big Dipper seem to make the shape of a dipper. Or saucepan. Three stars make the handle. Four stars make the bowl, the two stars that are at the front of the bowl are called "pointers." They are called "pointers" because they point to the North Star? When you look up at the North star, you are looking toward the north.

On Your Own

1. How many different ways can you say, "Good Morning"? Draw four pictures showing four different people you greet each morning. Under each picture, write the greeting you would use.

2. Sounds are all around you. Some sounds make you think of other sounds. Perhaps the drumming of fingers on a table top makes you think of the pitter-patter of rain hitting the window pane.

   Read each of these sentence beginnings. Write an ending for each of them.

   > The jet sounds like . . .
   > Water dripping from the faucet sounds like . . .
   > An alarm clock ticking sounds like . . .
   > Ice cubes hitting a glass sound like . . .
   > The clapping of hands sounds like . . .

3. Look at the pictures. Do they remind you of sounds, noises, or conversations you don't especially like? Make a list of sounds you don't like to hear.

4. Think of seven different animals. Write a sentence about each animal telling the sound each one makes. For example:

A horse neighs.

REVIEWS

When you give a review, you talk about yourself. You tell others what you think about a book you have read or a play you have seen. Share your opinion honestly. Other people want to hear it. It will help them decide what to read or what to see.

1 What to Tell About a Book

To Read and Think Over

When you have read a book and would like to share it with your friends, what should you tell them about it? Here is a book that Libby reviewed in class.

> *Pippi Longstocking,* by Astrid Lindgren, is a book about a girl named Pippi. Pippi is nine years old and lives with her monkey and her horse. She spends her time finding things, climbing trees, and playing with her friends. Pippi doesn't act like most children, so she gets into lots of trouble. My favorite part is when Pippi goes to the circus. She has a wrestling match with the strong man and wins! I like this book very much because Pippi always surprises me. If you want to read more about her adventures, *Pippi Longstocking* is in our classroom library.

 ● On your activity paper answer these questions.

1. What is the title of the book Libby reviewed?
2. Who wrote the book?
3. What was Libby's favorite part of the book?
4. Why did Libby like the book?

Talking Together

A. Discuss with your classmates the answers you wrote on your activity paper.

B. What did you learn about Pippi from this review? Would you like to learn more about her?

C. Is it a good idea to tell everything about a book to someone who hasn't read it yet? Why or why not?

D. Was Libby's book review a good one? Why or why not?

Follow these Guidelines when you review a book.

1. Tell the name of the book and the name of the author.
2. Tell what the book is about, but don't tell everything that happens.
3. Tell about one of the most interesting parts. If you like, you may read this part aloud.
4. Tell whether or not you liked the book and why.
5. Tell where your classmates can get the book.

To Do By Yourself

Think of a book you have read that you would like to review for your classmates. On a sheet of paper write the title and name of the author. Then write a sentence that tells why you liked or did not like the book.

2 Planning a Book Review

To Read and Think Over

It was Joseph's turn to give his book review to his class-mates. This is how he planned his review.

1. Joseph thought carefully about all the things he was going to tell in his review.
2. Joseph brought his book to class to show his classmates.
3. Joseph used a piece of paper to mark a place in the book that he wanted to read to his classmates.

Here is the way Joseph gave his review to the class.

1. Joseph spoke clearly.
2. Joseph tried to talk with expression.
3. Joseph showed the class his book. He read an exciting part of the book to his classmates.

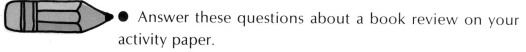 ● Answer these questions about a book review on your activity paper.

1. What should you think about ahead of time?
2. What should you mark in the book? How?
3. What should you do with the book during your review?

Talking Together

A. Discuss with your classmates the answers you wrote on your paper.

B. Did Joseph plan well for his book review? Why or why not?

Follow these Guidelines for planning and giving a book review.

1. **Plan your review ahead of time.**
2. **If you are going to read something from the book or show a picture, mark the place with a piece of paper.**

To Do By Yourself

Choose a book to review. Look at the pictures in this lesson or use the title of the book you chose in Lesson 1. Follow the GUIDELINES in this lesson in planning your review. Review the GUIDELINES on page 111 for what to tell in your review. Then take turns with your classmates in giving your book reviews. Answer any questions your classmates may have about your book.

3 Writing a Book Review

To Read and Think Over

Sometimes you may want to write a book review. A written review gives the same information as a spoken review.

Read Simon's review. Check the GUIDELINES for a book review. Did Simon follow them when he wrote his review?

Simon Ruland

Encyclopedia Brown Lends a Hand

This book is part of a series by Donald J. Sobol. Encyclopedia is the smartest boy in Idaville. He and Sally Kimball have a detective agency. Each chapter is about a different case. I liked the book because the solution to the mystery isn't given right away. You have a chance to guess it yourself. Then you find out if you guessed correctly. My favorite case was "The Case of the Frightened Witness." Encyclopedia and Sally had to figure out what the witness to a robbery was trying to tell them. If you want to try to figure it out, too, you can find this book in our school library.

 ● Answer these questions on your activity paper.

1. What is the title of the book?
2. Where did Simon place the title in the written book review?
3. Which words in the title begin with a capital letter?
4. Which words in the title have a line under them?

Talking Together

A. Discuss the answers you wrote on your activity paper.

B. Why is it useful to have a written book review? What are some ways your class might share written book reviews?

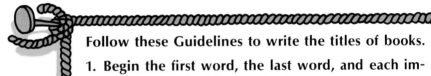

Follow these Guidelines to write the titles of books.

1. **Begin the first word, the last word, and each important word with a capital letter.**
2. **Words like <u>the</u>, <u>a</u>, <u>in</u>, and <u>to</u> are not considered important in a title.**
3. **Underline every word in the title.**

To Do By Yourself

Write the book review you told to your classmates in the last lesson, or choose another book to review. The GUIDELINES on page 111 will help you decide what to put in your book review. Follow the GUIDELINES in this lesson to write the title of your review correctly. After you have written your book review, proofread it. Make a new copy if you need to.

4 Using the Contents and Index

Contents

BEACON

To Read and Think Over

There are two parts in a book that tell you quickly what information the book contains. They are the **contents** and the **index.**

The contents is found in the front of a book. It lists all the titles of the chapters or units of the book and tells on what page each one begins.

The index is found at the end of a book. It lists in alphabetical order all the main topics in the book. It tells on what page or pages each topic is found. The index is much more detailed than the contents.

When you want to know if a book has information you need, look in the contents and the index to save time.

Study the index on page 117. The **main topics** are the important subjects in the book. They are listed in alphabetical order. Under each main topic there may be **subtopics.** A subtopic makes it easier to find exact information about a topic.

Africa, automobiles in, 219; bridges, 255; burdens carried by people, 314; burros, 331; railroads, 182, 185; roads, 210; wagons, 293

Airplanes, first, 8, 9 *p;* how controlled in the air, 15; how supported in the air, 16; how they came to be, 10–14; uses of, 63–72

Airports, in Canada, 97–98; in the United States, 70–72; on airmail routes, 65

Automobiles, different uses, for 217–219; how they came to be, 221–224; how they helped to improve roads, 207; increase in production, 227, 228 *t;* what the first ones were like, 224–226

first crossing of the *A*

Canals, George Washington's interest in, 2; in Canada, 350, 419; in Europe, 384, 385; in the United States, 380

Cargoes, how loaded and unloaded on ships, 382, 401; kinds of, 356–358, 362, 382, 401, 406, 409

Cars, early railroad, 105, 136; electric, 236–237; modern railroad, 109–117. *See also* **Pullman cars.**

Chicago, great railroad center, 117, 118 *m;* reached by foreign planes, 47; reached by ocean liners, 383

Coke. *See* **Fuel.**

Dirigible balloons, advantages of, 96; defined, 182; early experiments with, 83; how brought to earth   managed in

The main topic is sometimes followed by the words *see* or *see also* and the name of another topic. This tells you to look at another topic to find more information. This is a **cross-reference.**

 ● Write the answers to these questions on your activity paper.

1. In what part of a book do you find the contents?
2. What information do you find in the contents?
3. In what part of the book do you find the index?
4. What information do you find in an index?
5. In what order does an index list main topics?

Talking Together

A. Discuss the answers on your activity paper with your classmates. For what kinds of information would you look in the index? Why?

B. Not all books have a contents or an index. Can you think of one kind of book that does not need either? Why?

C. Why is it helpful to list topics in an index in alphabetical order?

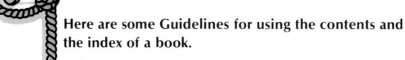

Here are some Guidelines for using the contents and the index of a book.

1. **The contents is in the front of a book. It lists chapters or units in order. It gives the pages for the beginning of each.**
2. **The index is at the end of a book. It lists all topics in the book in alphabetical order. It gives the pages where information for each topic can be found.**

To Do By Yourself

A. Use the contents in this book to answer these questions.
   1. What is the name of the first unit in this book? On what page does it begin?
   2. In what unit would you find information about giving reports? On what page does that unit begin?
   3. What is the name of Lesson 7 in Unit 6? On what page does that lesson begin?

B. Look in the index of this book to answer these questions.
   1. On what page or pages can you find information about thank-you letters?
   2. On what page or pages can you find information on giving directions?

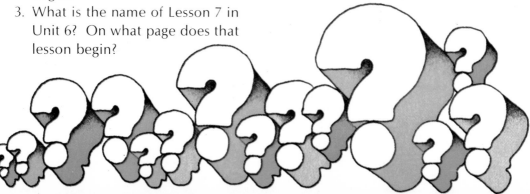

5 Using What You Have Learned

A. Think of a book you read and enjoyed. Write the title of the book and the author's name correctly. Write a paragraph that tells why you liked the book.

B. Here are the titles of four books. Review the GUIDELINES on page 115. Then write each book title correctly.

one hundred and eight bells
the cats stand accused
the goof that won the pennant
cyrus the unsinkable sea serpent

C. Copy this chart. Decide whether you would look in the contents or the index for this information. Place a check mark in the correct column.

CONTENTS	INDEX

1. titles of chapters in the book
2. page numbers on which chapters begin
3. an alphabetized list of main topics
4. a subtopic after a main topic
5. the cross reference to a main topic

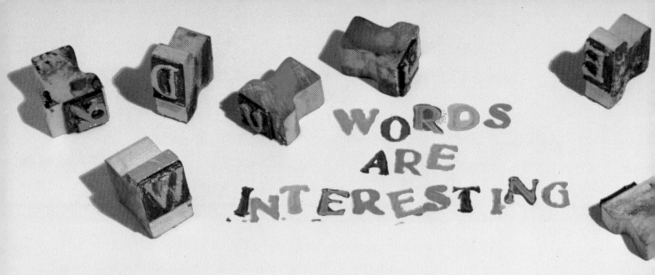

WORDS ARE INTERESTING

Choosing the Exact Noun

Words that are used to name something are called nouns. How *exactly* do you use nouns? For each word printed in dark letters, choose a word from the list that has the same number. Then copy the report and add the noun you chose.

The Koala

You probably have never seen a little **beast**[1] like the one in the picture because it lives only in Australia. It is called a koala. Many **people**[2] think it looks like a live **plaything.**[3] The gray **coat**[4] of a koala is soft and fluffy. The koala has large bushy ears and a big black **spot.**[5] Look at the **foot**[6] of the koala in the picture. Koalas live in **plants**[7] and their handlike paws make it easy for them to grasp the **limbs**[8] of trees as they climb.

Koalas never grow very large. The one in the picture is not a **baby.**[9] It is as large as it will ever be.

1	2	3	4	5
insect	girls	toy	fur	mark
bird	children	doll	hide	stripe
animal	boys	teddy bear	jacket	nose

6	7	8	9
toe	trees	leaves	cub
paw	weeds	branches	adult
arm	grass	roots	child

6 Learning About Verbs

To Read and Think Over

Look at these sentences. In each one, a word is printed in color. Each word in color is used to show action. Each one shows what someone or something **is doing.** Each one is a **verb.**

The girl runs.
Her kite flies.
Her cat watches.

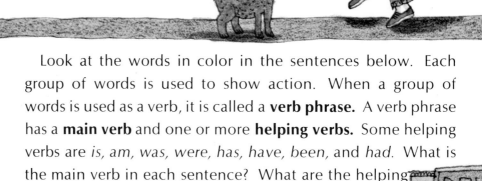

Look at the words in color in the sentences below. Each group of words is used to show action. When a group of words is used as a verb, it is called a **verb phrase.** A verb phrase has a **main verb** and one or more **helping verbs.** Some helping verbs are *is, am, was, were, has, have, been,* and *had.* What is the main verb in each sentence? What are the helping verbs?

The bus is stopping.
People are leaving the bus.
Other people have been waiting to get on.

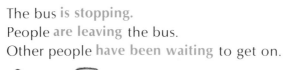

 ● Number your activity paper from 1 to 4. Find the verb or verb phrase in each sentence. Remember, a verb is a word or group of words that is used to show action. Copy the verb on your activity paper next to its numeral.

1. The package rattles.   3. I am opening it.
2. I have shaken it many times.   4. I tear the paper.

Talking Together

Discuss with your classmates the verbs you wrote on your activity paper. Did you choose the same words as your classmates?

> **Remember this Guideline about verbs.**
>
> **A word or group of words is a verb when it is used to show action.**

To Do By Yourself

A. Copy these sentences on your paper. Find the verb or verb phrase in each sentence. Draw a circle around the verb or verb phrase.

1. The cats meow.
2. The dogs are barking.
3. The choir will sing.
4. The wind was howling.
5. The tree branches shook.
6. The people were talking.
7. The bell rang three times.
8. It had been snowing.
9. Then it rained.
10. Now the sun is shining.

B. Add a verb or verb phrase to each group of words. Write each sentence on your paper.

1. Monica _____ the baby a cookie.
2. The baby _____ the cookie.
3. John had _____ the cookies.
4. The wind _____ the trees.
5. Lorrie was _____ a letter.
6. She _____ out of the window.
7. A dog _____ a cat in the yard.
8. Lorrie _____ the window.
9. She _____ the dog.
10. The dog _____.

7 Verbs and Their Tense

To Read and Think Over

There is one thing that only a verb can do. A verb can show the **time** when something happened. A verb changes form to show time gone by. Often the verb adds an ending to do this. Study this example.

> TODAY I play.
> YESTERDAY I played.

How did the verb *play* change to show time? Did you notice _-ed_ was added when the sentence started with *yesterday?*

Study the verbs on this chart. Watch the verb form change when the sentence talks about the past.

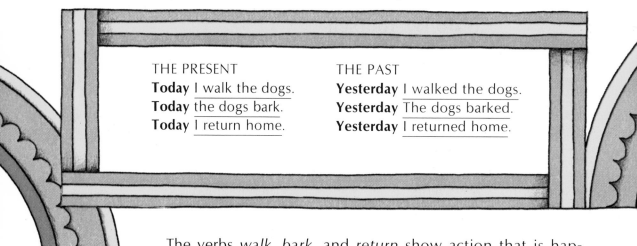

THE PRESENT	THE PAST
Today I walk the dogs.	**Yesterday** I walked the dogs.
Today the dogs bark.	**Yesterday** The dogs barked.
Today I return home.	**Yesterday** I returned home.

The verbs *walk, bark,* and *return* show action that is happening now. This verb form is called **present tense.**

The verbs *barked, walked,* and *returned* show action that happened in the past. This verb form is called **past tense.** Did you notice that _-ed_ was added to each verb? The ending _-ed_ is added to many verbs to show past tense.

 ● Number your activity paper from 1 to 4. Read each sentence. If the verb shows action that is happening now, write *present tense* beside the numeral of the sentence. If the verb shows action that already happened, write *past tense* next to the numeral of that sentence.

1. Ellen **entered** the room.
2. All trucks **turn** right at the corner.
3. I **listen** to footsteps.
4. We **walked** to the store.

Talking Together

A. Discuss the answers you wrote on your activity paper.

B. When a verb tells about action that is happening now, what is the verb form called?

C. When a verb tells about action that already happened, what is the verb form called?

D. What is the one thing that only a verb can do?

Follow these Guidelines for verbs.

1. **Verbs can change form to show a change in time.**
2. **Verbs in the present tense show what is happening now.**
3. **Verbs in the past tense show what has already happened. Many verbs add the ending ed to show past tense.**

To Do By Yourself

A. Change the time in each statement from present to past. Write the statements on your paper.
1. We pick pretty flowers.
2. The flowers smell nice.
3. We walk to school.
4. Jets land at the big airport.

B. Change the time in each statement from past to present. Write the statements on your paper.
1. They started running fast.
2. We collected stamps.
3. My sister and I washed the car.
4. My brothers played the drums.

8 The Special Verb Be

To Read and Think Over

Look at these pictures. Read the sentence under each one

Gary runs.   My name is Gary.

Look at the sentence on the left. The verb *runs* is a verb which shows action.

Look at the sentence on the right. The verb *is* does not show action. It simply shows that **something is,** or that **something exists.**

You have learned that most verbs show action. You will now learn about a special verb that does not show action. We call this special verb **be.** The verb *be* has many forms. Study the two charts on page 127. They show the present tense and past tense of *be.* Notice that there are many forms of this special verb.

PRESENT TENSE		PAST TENSE	
I am here.	We are here.	I was here.	We were here.
You are here.	You are here.	You were here.	You were here.
He is here.	They are here.	He was here.	They were here.
She is here.	They are here.	She was here.	They were here.
It is here.	They are here.	It was here.	They were here.

 ● On your activity paper copy these sentences. Circle the form of *be* used in each sentence.

Present Tense

1. It is very cold today.
2. We are ready for school.
3. Nancy is a girl.
4. Carlos is a boy.
5. You are late.
6. I am ten years old.

Past Tense

7. I was ten on my last birthday.
8. You were late.
9. They were clowns in the play.
10. She was a funny clown.

Talking Together

A. Discuss your sentences with your classmates. What are the present tense forms of the verb *be?* What are the past tense forms?

B. Work with a partner to practice the various forms of *be.* Here is a chart. Add a word or phrase such as *sad, happy,* or *a real superstar.*

PRESENT		PAST	
I am _____.	We are _____.	I was _____.	We were _____.
You are _____.	You are _____.	You were _____.	You were _____.
He is _____.	They are _____.	He was _____.	They were _____.
She is _____.	The guests are ____.	She was _____.	The guests were ___.

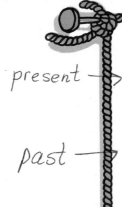

present →

past →

Follow these Guidelines when you use the verb <u>be</u>.
1. The present tense of <u>be</u> has three forms.
   <u>Am</u> is used with <u>I</u>.
   <u>Is</u> is used with <u>he</u>, <u>she</u>, <u>it</u>, and singular nouns.
   <u>Are</u> is used with <u>we</u>, <u>you</u>, <u>they</u>, and plural nouns.
2. The past tense of <u>be</u> has two forms.
   <u>Was</u> is used with the subject <u>I</u> and with <u>he</u>, <u>she</u>, <u>it</u>,
   and singular nouns.
   <u>Were</u> is used with <u>we</u>, <u>you</u>, <u>they</u>, and plural nouns.

To Do By Yourself

A. Number your paper from 1 to 10. Beside each numeral
write the correct <u>present</u> tense form for *be*.

They ___1___ at home.

We ___2___ outside.

I ___3___ nearby.

You ___4___ here.

She ___5___ here too.

He ___6___ here.

The school ___7___ there.

The toys ___8___ in your room.

You both ___9___ outside.

It ___10___ on the table.

B. Number your paper from 11 to 20. Beside each numeral
write the correct <u>past</u> tense form for *be*.

I ___11___ on my way.

You ___12___ already there.

He ___13___ ready.

Her friend ___14___ late.

She ___15___ on time.

It ___16___ nice to meet you.

They ___17___ glad too.

We ___18___ sad to go.

You both ___19___ here.

The booths ___20___ full.

128

9 Subjects and Predicates

To Read and Think Over

Look at these sentences. How are they divided?

SUBJECT	PREDICATE
1. The bus	stops here.
2. The people	waited in line.

Sentences have two parts, a **subject** and a **predicate.** The subject tells *who* or *what* is talked about in the sentence. The predicate tells *what this person or thing does or did.*

Find the subject of a sentence by asking *who* or *what.*

What is talked about in the first sentence?	The bus
Who is talked about in the second sentence?	The people

Find the predicate of a sentence by asking what the subject *does* or *did.* The first word in the predicate is usually a verb.

The bus **does what?**	stops here.
The people **did what?**	waited in line.

 ● Copy these sentences on your activity paper. Divide each one into two parts by drawing a line between the subject and the predicate.

1. Alvin Little is my cousin.
2. He lives next door to me.
3. My best friend moved away last week.
4. A new family moved into their apartment.

129

Talking Together

A. Discuss with your classmates the subjects and predicates you wrote.

B. Which part of a sentence usually comes first?

C. What questions did you ask yourself to help you find the subject of each sentence?

D. What questions did you ask to find each predicate?

E. Do subjects or predicates usually start with the verb?

Remember these **Guidelines** about subjects and predicates.

1. **All sentences have a subject and a predicate.**
2. **The subject tells <u>who</u> or <u>what</u> is talked about in the sentence.**
3. **The predicate tells something about the subject.**

To Do By Yourself

A. Copy these sentences on your paper. Divide each sentence into two parts by drawing a line between the subject and the predicate. Remember to look for the verb.

1. The Vikings came to America before Columbus.
2. They sailed across the Atlantic.
3. Whole families sailed together.
4. Their boats probably landed in Canada.
5. Old stone houses have been found in Newfoundland.

B. Add a subject to each predicate. Write each sentence on your paper.

1. _____ looked very sad.
2. _____ whizzed by.
3. _____ went swimming today.
4. _____ have long claws.
5. _____ came from the oven.

C. Add a predicate to these subjects. Write each sentence on your paper.

1. The big monsters _____.
2. A woman on horseback _____.
3. The pilot _____.
4. That book _____.
5. My best friend _____.

130

10 Simple Subjects

To Read and Think Over

The red car   drove by.

There is one word that is the most important word in the subject. This word is the **simple subject** of the sentence. In the sentence *The red car drove by* the simple subject is *car*.

Study these sentences. The simple subjects are in color.

Big trees   grow in the park.
My two friends   rode their bikes.

Trees is the simple subject of the first sentence. It is the most important word of the subject.

Friends is the simple subject of the second sentence. It is the most important word. Notice that the simple subject is usually a *noun*.

● Number your activity paper from 1 to 4. Find the simple subject of each sentence. Copy it next to its numeral.

1. An old woman is sitting by the window.
2. Two little girls waved to her.
3. A big cat is sitting beside her.
4. The noisy trucks drove down the street.

Talking Together

Discuss the answers you wrote on your activity paper with your classmates.

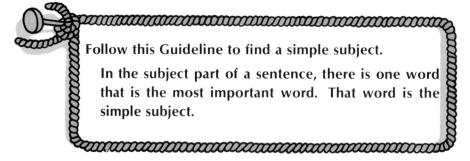

Follow this Guideline to find a simple subject.

In the subject part of a sentence, there is one word that is the most important word. That word is the simple subject.

To Do By Yourself

A. Copy each sentence. Draw one line under the simple subject of each sentence. The first sentence is done for you.

1. <u>Alma</u> heard about the fair.
2. Many people would be there.
3. She wanted to go.
4. Her best friend was going.
5. Alma's mother said yes.
6. Saturday was the big day.
7. The fairgrounds were crowded.
8. Suddenly a big van pulled up.
9. Four white horses stepped out.
10. The parade was about to begin!

B. Complete these sentences by adding a subject. Try to use more than one word for your subject. Copy each sentence on your paper. Then underline the simple subject in each sentence. Remember the simple subject is the most important word of the subject.

1. _____ blew.
2. _____ began the parade.
3. _____ followed close behind.
4. _____ marched two by two.
5. _____ played the drums.
6. _____ waved to the crowd.
7. _____ shouted and cheered.
8. _____ bobbed their balloons.
9. _____ stretched their necks.
10. _____ began to cry.

11 Simple Predicates

To Read and Think Over

Study these sentences. The verb in each sentence is printed in color.

The car   stops.
The car   had stopped for a red light.
The car   had been stopped a long time.

Did you notice that the verb in each of the sentences is located in the predicate part of the sentence? The verb is usually the first word or words in the predicate.

The simple subject is the most important word of the subject. The most important word or group of words in the predicate is the verb. The verb or verb phrase is the **simple predicate.**

● Number your activity paper from 1 to 5. Find the simple predicate in each of these sentences. Copy it on your activity paper next to the number of the sentence. Remember that the simple predicate is a verb. A verb can be more than one word.

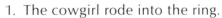

1. The cowgirl rode into the ring.
2. The crowd cheered loudly.
3. Her horse leaped into the air.
4. A trumpet sounded.
5. Everyone was waiting for the show to begin.

Talking Together

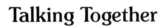

Discuss the answers you wrote on your activity paper with your classmates. Did you choose the same simple predicates as your classmates?

Follow this Guideline to find the simple predicate.

In the predicate part of the sentence, there is always a verb. The verb can be one word or a group of words. The verb always is the simple predicate of the sentence.

To Do By Yourself

A. Copy each sentence. Draw two lines under the simple predicate of each sentence.

1. The magician walked on stage.
2. The magician took a bow.
3. Ten rabbits jumped from his hat.
4. Everyone laughed.
5. The rabbits ran around the stage.
6. The magician tried to catch them.
7. The rabbits ran off the stage.
8. The curtain closed.
9. The rabbits ran back on stage.
10. He put them in their cage.

B. Complete these sentences by adding a predicate. Try to use more than one word for your predicate. Write the sentences on your paper. Then draw two lines under the simple predicate in each sentence.

1. Toby _____.
2. The boats _____.
3. A little sailboat _____.
4. The beautiful brown horse _____.
5. The hockey puck _____.
6. At the playground we _____.
7. A big silver jet _____.
8. The girls and boys _____.
9. Hotdogs and popcorn _____.
10. Tomorrow we _____.

12 Using What You Have Learned

A. Copy each sentence. Draw two lines under each verb.

1. My sister has been jogging.
2. She is joining the track team.

3. They are working in the gym.
4. We saw them yesterday.

B. Copy this chart. Complete it by writing the word that fits each space in this chart.

SUBJECT	PRESENT TENSE	PAST TENSE
I They You We	_____. walk. _____. jump.	looked. _____. stayed. _____.

C. Replace each space with a present tense form of *be*. Write each sentence on your paper.

1. Stephanie _____ the president.
2. We _____ ready to vote.

3. I _____ in line.
4. You _____ absolutely right.

D. Replace each space with a past tense form of *be*. Write each sentence on your paper.

1. The monkeys _____ in a cage.
2. Roger _____ at the zoo.

3. You _____ in the gift shop.
4. I _____ there, too.

E. Copy these sentences on your paper. Divide each sentence into two parts by drawing a line between the subject and predicate. Then draw one line under the simple subject, and two lines under the simple predicate.

1. Two families live in our house.
2. We live on the first floor.

3. The other family lives upstairs.
4. My grandparents are visiting us.

TRY IT AGAIN

Verbs (pages 122–128)

A. Complete these sentences on your paper, adding a verb.

1. My father _____ a new tent.
2. We _____ it to a new camping place.
3. We _____ in our sleeping bags.
4. Mosquitoes _____ us all night.
5. We _____ ten fish the next day.

B. Copy these sentences. In each statement, change the time from present to past by changing the form of the verb.

1. We ask many questions.
2. Our teachers always answer them.
3. We listen carefully.
4. They explain the answers clearly.
5. After lunch we play on the playground.

C. Copy these sentences. Change the time from past to present by changing the form of the verb.

1. We watched the new program.
2. The children showed their stamp collection.
3. They played with their racing cars.
4. The people enjoyed all the songs.
5. The children answered all the questions.

D. Write these sentences. Use the correct form for the present tense of *be*.

    1. Today you _____ in school.
    2. I _____ still studying.
    3. Tom _____ late for his class.
    4. Susan _____ home sick today.
    5. We _____ not home.

E. Write these sentences. Use the correct form for the past tense of *be*.

    1. Yesterday we _____ not at the playground.
    2. Tom _____ not there, either.
    3. I _____ home with a sore throat.
    4. They _____ home, too.
    5. _____ you at school?

Subjects and Predicates (pages 129–136)

Write these sentences on your paper. Divide each sentence into two parts by drawing a line between the subject and the predicate. Then draw one line under the simple subject, and two lines under the simple predicate.

    1. My father took us to the zoo.
    2. We went by subway.
    3. An attendant was feeding the animals.
    4. Several children gave the elephant popcorn.
    5. A little booth sold ice cream, cold drinks, and sandwiches.

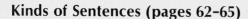

DO YOU REMEMBER ?

Kinds of Sentences (pages 62-65)

Copy each sentence. Add the correct end punctuation. Then show what kind of sentence each is by writing *S* for statement, *Q* for question, *C* for command, or *E* for exclamation.

1. Shut the window
2. The rain is coming in
3. What a loud clap of thunder
4. Don't be afraid of thunder
5. Do you like summer storms

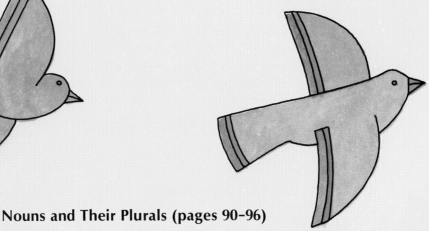

Nouns and Their Plurals (pages 90-96)

Number your paper from 1 to 10. Find and write the ten nouns in these sentences. Next to each noun, write its plural.

1. The latch on the door won't lock.
2. A crash made the fox drop the box.
3. That match lit the fire.
4. The witch made a guess about the riddle.

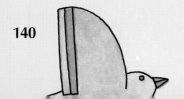

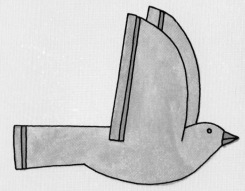

Proper and Common Nouns (pages 99–100)

Write these headings on your paper: *Common Nouns, Proper Nouns.* Find the nouns in the sentences below. List each one under the correct heading.

1. The girl went to Ottawa with her family.
2. They saw the Natural History Museum.
3. Mrs. McCabe took a picture of the building.
4. That bus will go to the National Arts Centre.

Using Correct Word Forms (pages 34–36)

Copy each sentence on your paper twice. First complete each sentence with the correct form of *is* or *are*. The second time, complete each one with *was* or *were*.

1. You _____ here early.
2. The girls _____ ready to leave for the trip.
3. The boys _____ late.
4. _____ the bus large enough?
5. The bus driver _____ ready to leave.

On Your Own

1. Write a review of your favorite magazine. These questions may be helpful.

   Do you like to look at the pictures?
   Do you read any of the stories?
   What parts do you like best?

2. You have been asked to review two television programs for your classmates. Write a review for each program. These questions may help you.

   Which two programs would you choose?
   What are they about?
   What days and times are they shown?
   Why do you think your classmates will like them?

3. Pretend you are a library book. Write a story or a report about some of the things that have happened to you. These questions may help you.

> How long have you been in the library?
> Who are some of the people that have read you?
> Did they handle you gently?
> Did they lose you, or did they return you to the library?

4. In *The Wizard of Oz,* no one on the farm expected a tornado. And Dorothy never expected to find herself in the Land of Oz after the tornado swept by.

   Read this list of things that we would never expect to happen. Choose one of them and write a story which will tell what might happen if this change took place.

> If your car became invisible
> If you could turn off gravity, and everything floated in air
> If your dog started talking
> If the oceans dried up
> If your house turned into an airplane

DIRECTIONS

When people ask you for directions, be very exact. Tell them which way to go and how far to go. Tell them where and when to turn. Tell them what to look for along the way. If you give exact directions, people will be happy they asked you.

1 What to Tell in Directions

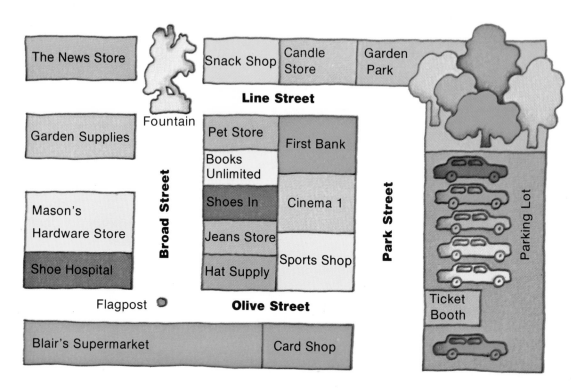

To Read and Think Over

James told his friend Mark how to go from Mason's Hardware Store to the Candle Store. Can you follow his directions?

When you leave Mason's Hardware Store, you will be on Broad Street. Turn left on Broad Street and walk toward the fountain. When you reach the fountain, you'll see that you're on the corner of Broad Street and Line Street. Turn right on Line Street. The Candle Store is the second store on the left side.

Notice the way James gave his directions. He began at the exact place where Mark would start. He told Mark which way to turn. He told Mark to look for something special, the fountain. He told his directions in order, one step at a time.

 ● Use the map of the shopping center to help Susan go from the Candle Store to the Shoe Hospital. Write the directions on your activity paper. Follow this form.

When you leave The Candle Store, you will be on Line Street. Turn _____ on Line Street. Walk toward the _____ on the corner of _____ and _____ Streets. Turn _____ onto _____ Street. Pass the Garden Supplies Store and _____. The Shoe Hospital is the _____ store on your _____.

Talking Together

A. Discuss the directions you wrote.

B. Use the map to give two ways that someone could go from the Candle Store to the Card Shop.

C. A fountain is a **landmark.** A landmark *marks land* in a special way. How does a landmark help a person to follow directions?

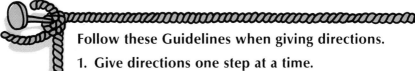

Follow these Guidelines when giving directions.

1. **Give directions one step at a time.**
2. **Tell each step in the right order.**
3. **Make each direction clear. Tell exactly where to turn and how far to go.**
4. **Point out landmarks the person will see.**

To Do By Yourself

A. Draw a map of your neighborhood. Label the streets and buildings. Here are some of the places you might include on your map.

　your house　　　some stores
　the fire station　a friend's house

B. Then write directions from your house to one of the places on the map. Be sure to follow the GUIDE-LINES in this lesson.

2 Giving Instructions

To Read and Think Over

Johanna's brother asked her how he could start growing an avocado plant. She wrote these instructions for him.

How to Start an Avocado Plant

Materials needed:

A ripe avocado   Four toothpicks   A glass

Steps to follow:

1. Have someone cut the avocado in half the long way.
2. Separate the avocado pit from the fruit.
3. Insert four toothpicks about halfway down the pit.
4. Set the avocado pit in a glass so that the toothpicks rest on the top of the glass.
5. Cover the bottom of the avocado pit with water.
6. Set the glass in a warm, partly dark place. Keep the bottom of the pit covered with water. Roots will start growing in a week or two.

● On your activity paper answer these questions.

1. Where did Johanna list the materials needed to start an avocado plant?
2. Did Johanna list the instructions one step at a time?

Talking Together

A. Discuss the answers you wrote on your activity paper.

B. Think of something you know how to build or make. Do you know how to make a scrapbook or put a model car together? Can you explain how to make your favorite dessert? Discuss the materials needed and the steps necessary to complete your project.

When you give instructions, follow these Guidelines.

1. **Tell what materials are needed.**
2. **Give instructions one step at a time.**
3. **Make each step clear. Use exact words.**
4. **Give the steps in the order they should be done.**

To Do By Yourself

Write a set of instructions. Use one of the topics that you discussed in this lesson. Follow the GUIDELINES for writing instructions. Make some drawings to show how the steps are to be done. Proofread your work.

3 Directions for Using the Dictionary

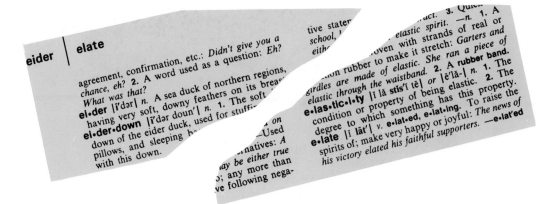

To Read and Think Over

A dictionary is a special book about words. It can give you many kinds of information about words. To use a dictionary, you must follow certain directions.

Words are listed in alphabetical order in the dictionary. Learn to open the dictionary to the **front, middle,** or **back** according to the first letter of the word you are looking for.

The **guide words** on top of each page tell you whether or not a word is on a particular page. The guide word on the left stands for the first word on the page. The guide word on the right stands for the last word on the page.

Look up the **base word** if your word has a common ending, such as *-ing, -ly, -ed,* or *-s* added to it. A base word is a word that may be used alone, before a common ending is added. For example, the base word for *borrowing* is *borrow.*

 ● Copy the chart on page 151 on your activity paper. Write the base words in the correct space for numerals 2 to 5. The first one is done for you.

© 1972, 1977, Houghton Mifflin Company. Reprinted by permission from *The American Heritage School Dictionary.*

THE WORD YOU READ	THE BASE WORD
1. mixed	mix
2. complaining	————
3. loosely	————
4. pierces	————
5. tallest	————

Talking Together

A. Discuss with your classmates the answers you wrote on your paper.

B. What are guide words? How do they help you use a dictionary?

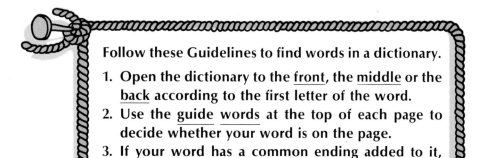

Follow these Guidelines to find words in a dictionary.

1. Open the dictionary to the <u>front</u>, the <u>middle</u> or the <u>back</u> according to the first letter of the word.
2. Use the <u>guide words</u> at the top of each page to decide whether your word is on the page.
3. If your word has a common ending added to it, drop the ending and look up the base word.

To Do By Yourself

For each of these words, write the word you would look for in the dictionary. If the word is already in its base form, write it as it is. If the word has an ending added to it, write just the base word.

1. cocoa
2. gilt
3. played
4. politely
5. harvest
6. always
7. stated
8. fade
9. games
10. charging

4 Directions for Pronouncing Words

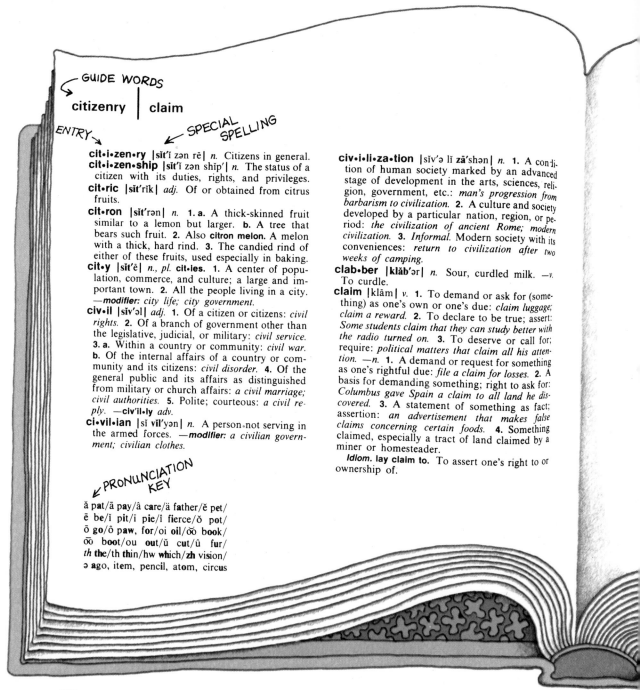

GUIDE WORDS

citizenry | claim

ENTRY

SPECIAL SPELLING

cit·i·zen·ry |sĭt′ĭ zən rē| *n.* Citizens in general.
cit·i·zen·ship |sĭt′ĭ zən shĭp′| *n.* The status of a citizen with its duties, rights, and privileges.
cit·ric |sĭt′rĭk| *adj.* Of or obtained from citrus fruits.
cit·ron |sĭt′rən| *n.* **1. a.** A thick-skinned fruit similar to a lemon but larger. **b.** A tree that bears such fruit. **2.** Also **citron melon.** A melon with a thick, hard rind. **3.** The candied rind of either of these fruits, used especially in baking.
cit·y |sĭt′ē| *n., pl.* **cit·ies. 1.** A center of population, commerce, and culture; a large and important town. **2.** All the people living in a city. —*modifier: city life; city government.*
civ·il |sĭv′əl| *adj.* **1.** Of a citizen or citizens: *civil rights.* **2.** Of a branch of government other than the legislative, judicial, or military: *civil service.* **3. a.** Within a country or community: *civil war.* **b.** Of the internal affairs of a country or community and its citizens: *civil disorder.* **4.** Of the general public and its affairs as distinguished from military or church affairs: *a civil marriage; civil authorities.* **5.** Polite; courteous: *a civil reply.* —*civ′il·ly adv.*
ci·vil·ian |sĭ vĭl′yən| *n.* A person not serving in the armed forces. —*modifier: a civilian government; civilian clothes.*

PRONUNCIATION KEY

ă pat/ā pay/â care/ä father/ĕ pet/
ē be/ĭ pit/ī pie/î fierce/ŏ pot/
ō go/ô paw, for/oi oil/oŏ book/
oō boot/ou out/ŭ cut/û fur/
th the/th thin/hw which/zh vision/
ə ago, item, pencil, atom, circus

civ·i·li·za·tion |sĭv′ə lĭ zā′shən| *n.* **1.** A condition of human society marked by an advanced stage of development in the arts, sciences, religion, government, etc.: *man's progression from barbarism to civilization.* **2.** A culture and society developed by a particular nation, region, or period: *the civilization of ancient Rome; modern civilization.* **3.** *Informal.* Modern society with its conveniences: *return to civilization after two weeks of camping.*
clab·ber |klăb′ər| *n.* Sour, curdled milk. —*v.* To curdle.
claim |klām| *v.* **1.** To demand or ask for (something) as one's own or one's due: *claim luggage; claim a reward.* **2.** To declare to be true; assert: *Some students claim that they can study better with the radio turned on.* **3.** To deserve or call for; require: *political matters that claim all his attention.* —*n.* **1.** A demand or request for something as one's rightful due: *file a claim for losses.* **2.** A basis for demanding something; right to ask for: *Columbus gave Spain a claim to all land he discovered.* **3.** A statement of something as fact; assertion: *an advertisement that makes false claims concerning certain foods.* **4.** Something claimed, especially a tract of land claimed by a miner or homesteader.
Idiom. **lay claim to.** To assert one's right to or ownership of.

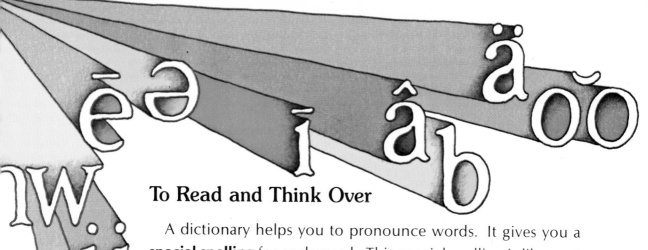

To Read and Think Over

A dictionary helps you to pronounce words. It gives you a **special spelling** for each word. This special spelling is like a set of directions. It tells exactly how to say the word.

Sam looked up the word *bauble* in the dictionary to find out how to pronounce it. This is what he found.

bau·ble |bô′bəl|

The black dot told Sam that *bauble* has two parts or two syllables. Then Sam looked at the special spelling for each syllable. Each vowel had a **diacritical mark** over it. Sam used the **pronunciation key** at the bottom of the page to find what sound each diacritical mark stands for.

Look at the special spelling of *bauble*. Then look at the pronunciation key. Which key word has the same vowel sound as the vowel sound in the first syllable? How is the vowel in the second syllable pronounced?

 ● Find the word *citric* on the sample dictionary page. Study the special spelling. Then write the answers to these questions on your activity paper.

1. How many syllables does *citric* have?
2. What letter is used in the special spelling to stand for the sound of c in the first syllable? What letter is used to stand for the sound of c in the second syllable?
3. What word in the pronunciation key tells you how to pronounce the vowel in the first syllable?

153

Talking Together

A. Discuss the answers you wrote on your activity paper.

B. How should these words be pronounced? If you are not sure of the correct pronunciation, check your dictionary.

gauge   lieu   corps   newt   sieve   ewe

> Remember these Guidelines when you use the dictionary to find out how to pronounce a word.
>
> 1. The syllables of a word are usually separated by a black dot.
> 2. The special spelling tells you how to pronounce each word in the dictionary.
> 3. The pronunciation key tells you what sound each diacritical mark stands for.

To Do By Yourself

Here are some words as you might see them in a dictionary. Under each word are some questions. Write the answer to each question on your paper.

A. an·tique |ăn tēk'| Something very old.
1. Which syllable is stressed?
2. What key word has the same vowel sound as the vowel sound in the stressed syllable?

B. de·light |dĭ līt'| To please very much.
1. What key word has the same vowel sound as the vowel sound in the first syllable?
2. What key word has the same vowel sound as the vowel sound in the second syllable?

5 Using What You Have Learned

A. Think of a place near your home or school. Write directions telling how to get to that place from either home or school. Review the GUIDELINES for giving directions on page 147.

B. Do you know how to make a birdhouse, bake a cake, or make a picture frame? Write a set of instructions that would tell someone else how to do it. Review the GUIDELINES on page 149.

C. Complete this chart.

A WORD YOU READ	THE BASE WORD
carelessly	
roughest	
joined	
painting	
encourages	
exhausted	
monkeys	
jumped	
reaching	
misspelled	

WORDS ARE INTERESTING

Verb Game

The words in the flowers on page 157 can be used as verbs. That is, they can be used to show actions.

How *exactly* do you use verbs? Find out by playing this game with your classmates.

1. Close your eyes and put your finger on the verb-flower page. Then, from the flower nearest your finger, choose one of the four verbs and write it on your paper. Do this two more times. You should have three verbs on your paper. Each verb should be from a different flower.

2. Now the sentence race begins! When your teacher tells you, write each verb you chose in a sentence of your own. You may use your dictionary to check meanings. Be sure to use the verb to tell *exactly* what something or someone does. Stop when your teacher says to.

3. When the time is up, players can read their sentences aloud. Other players can use the dictionary to check meanings.

157

6 Introducing Personal Pronouns

To Read and Think Over

A **pronoun** is a word used in place of a noun. Think of your own name. What pronoun do you use to take the place of your own name? Here are two examples.

> I came to school today.
> The teacher is talking to me.

I and **me** are **personal pronouns** that take the place of your name. Most personal pronouns stand for people's names, but *it* stands for a thing, a place, or an animal. *They* or *them* may stand for any plural noun, or for two or more nouns joined by *and.* Study this list of personal pronouns.

SINGULAR	PLURAL
I, me	we, us
you	you
he, she, it	they
him, her	them

 ● Number your activity paper from 1 to 11. Then read the conversation between Jane and Toby. Find eleven personal pronouns. List them on your activity paper.

Jane: Toby, have you seen Marguerite? She said she would be back with the skates in four minutes. I need them to practice this afternoon at the rink.

Toby: I saw her skating at the pond earlier today with Sam. They skated for about an hour and then he left. We should be seeing her soon.

Talking Together

A. Discuss the personal pronouns you listed on your paper.

B. Read the personal pronouns listed on page 158. Which pronouns would you use if you were talking about yourself and another person? Which one for your sister? Which one for three other people? Take turns with your classmates making up sentences using each pronoun.

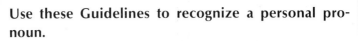

Use these Guidelines to recognize a personal pronoun.

1. **A personal pronoun is a word that is used in place of a noun.**
2. **The words in this list are personal pronouns.**

I, me	we, us
you	you
he, she, it	they
him, her	them

To Do By Yourself

Read these sentences. Replace the underlined words with a personal pronoun. Write each sentence on your paper.

1. The man swept the floor.
2. Then Shirley washed the floor.
3. Frankie and I wrote to Pauline.
4. Pauline answered right away.
5. Ralph and Marlon had a surprise.
6. The message was from Ralph and Marlon.
7. First Phyllis called Uncle Lou.
8. Then Uncle Lou called Phyllis.
9. Phyllis called the children.
10. The children talked with Phyllis.
11. Can Jim come?
12. Michel and I will be there.
13. Are the twins coming too?
14. When will Libby be ready?
15. Can you bring the pumpkin?

7 Using I and Me

To Read and Think Over

When you are speaking about another person and yourself, should you name yourself or the other person first?

I and **me** are used correctly in these sentences. Read them and see if you can tell why.

1. **Jennie and I** went to the movies.
2. Her dad drove **Jennie and me** there.
3. **Peter and I** will visit later.
4. **Jennie, Peter, and I** went to the park.
5. My aunt took my **sister and me** shopping.

Did you notice that when you speak of another person and yourself, you name the other person or persons first? Notice that *I* or *me* is last.

Look at the sentences on page 161 again. Sentence 1 used *Jennie and I*. Sentence 2 used *Jennie and me*. How do you know which form to use? Here is an easy way to be sure you use *I* or *me* correctly with another person's name. Simply cross out the other person's name. Leave your own name. Then decide whether to use *I* or *me* in each sentence. Which one sounds correct? Use that form. Then add the other person's name to the sentence again.

~~Jennie and~~ I went to the movies.
Her dad drove ~~Jennie and~~ me there.
~~Peter and~~ I will visit later.
~~Jennie, Peter, and~~ I went to the park.
My aunt took ~~my sister and~~ me shopping.

 ● Copy these sentences on your activity paper. Complete the sentences with *Andrew and I* or *Andrew and me*.

1. _____ decided to make a snow fort.
2. First _____ packed down the snow.
3. Tanner saw _____ and asked if she could help.
4. She helped _____ build the fort.

Talking Together

A. Discuss your sentences with your classmates.

B. Read these sentences with your classmates. Choose the correct group of words.

1. (Bernard and I, Bernard and me) went for a walk.
2. (I and Bella, Bella and I) will call you later.
3. This letter is for (Tony and me, me and Tony).
4. Mrs. Saunders took a picture of (Dwight and I, Dwight and me).

Follow these Guidelines when you use I and me.

1. **When you speak of yourself and others, name yourself last. Lee and I**
2. **When you speak of yourself and others, use I and me correctly. To make sure you have chosen the correct form, use I or me alone in the sentence.**

To Do By Yourself

Copy this story. Use either *Greta and I* or *Greta and me* in place of each space.

Dennis showed _____ a magic trick. _____ watched him hold up a handkerchief by the corner. Then he told _____ he was going to tie a knot by magic. _____ saw him pick up the other corner of the handkerchief. He asked _____ to say three magic words. _____ said the magic words. Dennis shook out the handkerchief for _____. In the corner _____ saw a knot.

8 Using Good and Well

You throw **well**.

That was a **good** catch.

To Read and Think Over

Read these sentences. The words **good** and **well** are used correctly in them.

1. Jimmy has a **good** pair of skates.
2. He can skate **well** in them.
3. June is a **good** swimmer.
4. She also dives very **well**.

Notice that the word *good* tells what kind of person or thing is being described. The word *well* tells how a person or thing acts or how something is being done.

Sometimes people say *good* when they should say *well*. Remember, it is not correct to use the word *good* after something you do. Anything you do, you do *well*.

 ● Copy these sentences on your activity paper. Replace each space with *good* or *well*.

1. Leo is a _____ speaker.
2. He also sings _____.
3. In our last discussion, he spoke _____.

4. He gave some _____ reasons for having school only four days a week.

Talking Together

A. Discuss the sentences you wrote with your classmates.

B. Close your book and listen while your teacher reads these sentences. Listen to *good* and *well* used correctly.

1. This is a _____ time to go to the lake.
2. We can plan our trip_____.
3. How _____ do you like fishing?
4. What are some _____ things to do?
5. Can you swim _____?

6. Martin is a _____ swimmer.
7. Sarah rides horseback very _____.
8. There are many _____ games we can play.
9. It is _____ to plan ahead.
10. Then we will use our time _____.

Follow these Guidelines when you use <u>good</u> and <u>well</u>.

1. The word <u>good</u> is used to tell what kind of person, place, or thing is being described.
   She is a <u>good</u> tennis player.
2. The word <u>well</u> is used to tell how a person or things acts or how something is done.
   She plays <u>well</u>.

To Do By Yourself

A. Copy the sentences your teacher read aloud from *Talking Together.* Use the correct word, *good* or *well,* in each space.

B. Copy this story. Use *good* or *well* correctly in place of each space.

Twinky is a _____ kitten. He is _____ at doing things a kitten should. He climbs trees _____. He is a _____ climber when he is going up. But he does not climb as _____ on the way down.

9 Using Two, Too, To; Their, There

To Read and Think Over

The words **two, too,** and **to** sound alike, but they have different meanings. Read these sentences in which *two, too,* and *to* are used correctly.

TWO ducks swim in the pond.

Suddenly it is TOO cold for them.

They start TO fly TO a warmer place.

The word *two* is a number. Count the ducks.

The word *too* means "more than enough." There is *more than enough* cold weather.

The word *to* can be used in different ways.

Two more words that sound alike but have different meanings are **their** and **there**. Read these sentences in which *their* and *there* are used correctly.

Joan and David put THEIR books on the table.   They left them THERE.

There is often used to tell in what place. *Their* is used to show that something belongs to more than one person or animal.

 ● Copy each sentence on your activity paper. Add the correct word in each space.

to, two, too

1. Please give me _____ pencils.
2. I would like some paper _____.
3. We can make a get-well card to send _____ Janet.
4. Let's give it _____ her tomorrow.
5. Then Rick and George can sign it _____.

their, there

6. The package was left _____.
7. It has _____ names on the label.
8. _____ hats are in the package.
9. Should we leave them _____?
10. Put this with the rest of _____ packages.

Talking Together

Discuss your sentences with your classmates.

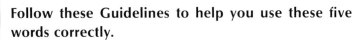

Follow these Guidelines to help you use these five words correctly.

1. The word <u>two</u> is a number.

   I ate <u>two</u> apples.

   The word <u>too</u> means "also" or "more than enough."

   I want a peach <u>too</u>. (also)

   This peach is <u>too</u> ripe. (more than enough)

   The word <u>to</u> has many different meanings.

   She went <u>to</u> her room <u>to</u> get the lock <u>to</u> her bicycle at five minutes <u>to</u> six.

2. The word <u>their</u> means "belonging to" or "owned by" more than one person or animal.

   The puppies wagged <u>their</u> tails.

   The word <u>there</u> has a number of different meanings. Often it means "in" or "at that place."

   <u>There</u> is my baseball glove.

   Put it <u>there</u>.

   <u>There</u> is no mail delivery today.

To Do By Yourself

Copy these paragraphs. Choose the correct word from the words in parentheses.

There is going to be an International Fair on Saturday. (Two, too, to) of my friends are going to wear (there, their) native dress. Kristen is going to bake cookies (two, too, to). She and I will go (two, too, to) the fair together.

Before we arrive (there, their), though, we will go to her grandparents' house. They are letting us use (there, their) slides of Sweden to show at the fair.

They have (two, too, to) boxes of slides taken during (there, their) stay (there, their) last year. They were visiting (there, their) relatives (there, their).

10 Sentence Pattern 1

To Read and Think Over

You have learned that when we use sentences that contain a noun plus a verb, we call these sentences the **N V pattern.**

$$\overset{\textbf{N}}{\text{Robins}} \overset{\textbf{V}}{\text{chirp.}} \qquad \overset{\textbf{N}}{\text{Ducks}} \overset{\textbf{V}}{\text{quack.}}$$

You can add one or more helping verbs without changing the sentence pattern.

$$\overset{\textbf{N}}{\text{Rain}} \overset{\textbf{V}}{\text{is falling.}} \qquad \overset{\textbf{N}}{\text{The children}} \overset{\textbf{V}}{\text{have been swimming.}}$$

 ● On your activity paper copy each of these sentences. Use <u>N</u> and <u>V</u> to show the pattern.

1. Girls sang.
2. Maria has been running.
3. Ben is crying.
4. The airplane is landing.

Talking Together

A. Discuss the sentences you wrote on your activity paper.

B. Add nouns or verbs to complete these sentences.

1. __N__ is talking.
2. The bus has __V__ .
3. Tina __V.__ .
4. __N__ is smiling.

Follow this Guideline.

<u>NV</u> is a sentence pattern. It stands for <u>noun plus verb.</u>

To Do By Yourself

Use the N V pattern to write ten sentences of your own.

11 Subject and Verb Agreement

To Read and Think Over

You know that a verb can tell what one person or thing is doing. A verb can also tell what two or more persons or things are doing.

Read these sentences. The verb forms *work* and *works* are used correctly. Which verb form tells about only one person or thing? Which form tells about more than one?

1. Dad **works** in a store all week.
2. They **work** around the house.
3. Sometimes I **work** with them.
4. Mom **works** in an office in town.
5. Mom, Dad, and I **work** in our yard.
6. You **work** in your yard too.

Works is used with a singular noun or the pronoun *he, she,* or *it. Works* is the verb form that ends in *-s.*

● Copy these sentences on your activity paper. Use the verb form that agrees with the subject.

1. Jill (walk, walks) to her Saturday classes.
2. Sometimes we (drive, drives) her home.
3. She (want, wants) to learn how to speak Spanish.
4. Carla (help, helps) her to speak it.
5. They (talk, talks) a lot during recess.

Talking Together

A. Discuss your sentences with your classmates.

B. Close your book and listen while your teacher reads these sentences. Listen to hear the verb forms used correctly.

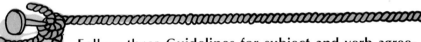

1. Our grandparents (own, owns) a new red car.
2. It (start, starts) quickly on cold days.
3. Grandfather (ask, asks) me if I want a ride sometimes.
4. He (show, shows) me how he follows driving directions.
5. My brother and I (feel, feels) proud of him.
6. He (know, knows) a lot about new cars.
7. He (call, calls) Grandma a better driver.
8. Sometimes she (test, tests) him about the parts of a car.
9. The new car (climb, climbs) hills safely in the winter.
10. It (run, runs) well in every kind of weather.

Follow these **Guidelines** for subject and verb agreement.

1. Use the -<u>s</u> form of a verb when the subject is a singular noun or the pronoun <u>she</u>, <u>he</u>, or <u>it</u>.
2. Never use the -<u>s</u> form of a verb when the subject is the pronoun <u>you</u>, whether <u>you</u> stands for one or more than one person.

To Do By Yourself

Copy each sentence from *Talking Together*. Use the verb that agrees with the subject.

12 Using What You Have Learned

A. Use a personal pronoun in place of every underlined word in this story. Write the story on your paper. The GUIDE-LINES on page 160 may help you.

Rita and I know a girl named Ella. One day Ella had a great idea. The idea was to hunt for treasure. She asked Rita and me to call all our friends. We called our friends, and our friends came over right away. Then I asked Ella if I could invite my brother too. She told me to get my brother. My brother joined my friends and me for the treasure hunt.

B. Copy these sentences. Choose the correct words from the words in parentheses.

1. (Perry and I, Perry and me) went to a play.
2. An usher helped (Perry and I, Perry and me) find our seats.
3. He gave (Perry and I, Perry and me) our programs.
4. (Perry and I, Perry and me) thought they were hard to read in the dark.
5. A flashlight would have been a big help to (Perry and I, Perry and me).

C. Copy this story on your paper. Write either *good* or *well* in place of each space.

1. There is a _____ art show at school.
2. Most of the paintings are done very _____.
3. Jean did hers especially _____.
4. She uses many different colors _____.
5. The painting she made of the girl has _____ color in it.
6. Tom draws _____.
7. My sister is a _____ skater.
8. She is teaching me to skate _____.
9. She can spin _____ on skates.
10. Maybe someday I'll be able to skate _____ too.

D. Write two sentences of your own for each of these words: *two, to, too, their,* and *there.*

173

Personal Pronouns (pages 158–160)

Use a personal pronoun in place of every underlined word in this story. Write the story on your paper.

Our family took a day trip to the mountains. Before we left, Dad gave <u>Jane, Bill, and me</u> each one dollar for spending money. <u>Dad</u> said we could spend <u>the dollar</u> any way we wanted to. Jane saw an Indian basket in a store window. <u>Jane</u> spent almost all her money on <u>the basket</u>. Bill and I told <u>Jane</u> to save the rest for ice cream.

Correct Word Forms (pages 161–168)

A. Copy these sentences. Put **Sherry and I** or **Sherry and me** in each space.

1. Mom gave _____ two tickets for the ball game.
2. _____ had never been to a major league game before.
3. When _____ got there, it began to rain.
4. An umbrella would have been a big help for _____.
5. Next time _____ go to a ball game, we will listen to the weather report first.

B. Copy these sentences. Write either *good* or *well* in place of the blank.

1. Sue is a _____ ballplayer.
2. She bats _____.
3. She also runs as _____ as anyone on the team.
4. Roberto is a _____ catcher.
5. He doesn't hit _____.

C. Copy these sentences. Choose the correct word from the words in parentheses.

1. (Two, too, to) of my friends went to the movies yesterday.
2. They went to see (there, their) favorite movie star.
3. My brother and I will go tomorrow (two, too, to).
4. Before we go (there, their), we plan to visit our grandmother.
5. Mr. and Mrs. Nelson and (there, their) children lived (two, too, to) miles from me.
6. I used to ride my bike over (there, their) when the weather wasn't (two, too, to) bad.
7. They had moved (two, too, to) far away for me (two, too, to) do that.

Sentence Pattern 1 (page 169)

Add a noun or a verb to complete each sentence.

1. _____ is dancing.
2. _____ sings.
3. The puppies _____.
4. The sun _____.

Subject and Verb Agreement (pages 170–171)

Copy these sentences. Use the verb form that agrees with the subject.

1. This orange (taste, tastes) sweet.
2. Oranges (grow, grows) in this grove.
3. The man (pick, picks) them from the tree.
4. Then he (pack, packs) the oranges in boxes.
5. The girl (help, helps) pack them.

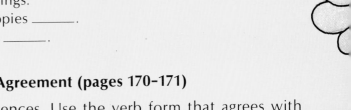

175

DO YOU REMEMBER ?

Subjects and Predicates (pages 129–136)

Copy each sentence. Divide each sentence into two parts by drawing a line between the subject and the predicate. Then draw one line under the simple subject, and two lines under the simple predicate.

1. Mr. Riley's class planted some flower seeds.
2. Spring came.
3. All the beautiful flowers bloomed at once.
4. Our teacher took a picture of them.
5. The newspaper used the picture.
6. The weeds grew quickly.
7. My brother's class planted vegetable seeds.
8. They grew carrots and lettuce.
9. The children weeded the garden during the summer.
10. Some rabbits ate a few carrots.

Possessive Nouns (pages 97-98)

Write each sentence, using the correct possessive form in parentheses.

1. Her (dog's, dogs') name is Ladybug.
2. The two (girl's, girls') mother is looking for Ladybug's puppies.
3. Where are the four (puppy's, puppies') collars?
4. Father brought (Sue's, Sues') dog a bone.
5. All four (dog's, dogs') collars were found.

Verbs and Their Tenses (pages 124-128)

Copy these sentences. Change the time in each sentence from past to present by changing the tense of the verb.

1. Bill and Mike collected stamps from many countries.
2. We looked at their collection.
3. Two stamps were from Germany.
4. They wanted some stamps from France.
5. They enjoyed their hobby very much.

Common and Proper Nouns (pages 99-100)

Write these headings on your paper: *Common Nouns, Proper Nouns.* Find the nouns in the sentences below. Write each one under the correct heading.

1. The family went to Oregon on a plane.
2. Lou and Linda saw the Rocky Mountains.
3. The pilot talked about Lake Tahoe.
4. Many houses stood around the lake.

On Your Own

1. What is your favorite food? How do you cook it? Write the recipe. First list all the ingredients and how much of each one you need. Then write the steps needed to prepare the dish.

2. When you were younger, there were many things you didn't know how to do. Write a story telling about something you didn't know how to do, but know how to do now. Look at the pictures. They may give you some ideas.

178

3. You left your baseball glove under your bed. Write directions that would help a friend find his or her way from the front door of your house to your bedroom.

4. How do you care for a pet? What does the pet eat? What shouldn't the pet eat? How do you keep the pet clean? What safety steps should you take?

Make a chart on your paper. In the first column write all the things you must do for this pet. In the second column write all the things you should not do for this pet. Be sure to write in sentences.

STORIES AND POEMS

Everyone loves a good story or poem. If you plan yours carefully and tell it in an interesting way, others will enjoy it. Tell a story. Make up a play or song that tells a story. Read a poem aloud. Enjoy other people's stories and poems. They will enjoy yours, too!

1 Talking About Stories

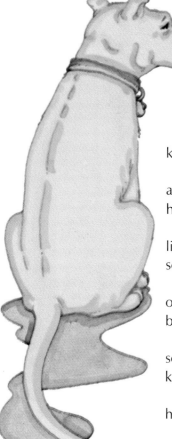

The Poltergeist
Betty Boegehold

"Listen! What's that creaking noise?" whispered Trina.

"I don't hear anything. Quit stalling, Trina," said Cam, "You know if we don't get our homework done, we can't watch TV."

"I'm not stalling," insisted Trina. "Listen! There's the noise again. I'm really scared." It was Trina's first time away from home. She was spending the night at Cam's house.

"I'm listening," said Cam. "But all I hear is the radio in the living room and the dog scratching. When my dog itches, he scratches."

"No, no!" whispered Trina. "I heard something else. A kind of scratching, scrabbling sound. Listen again. And don't breathe too loudly."

Cam listened again. And this time she DID hear a small scratching, scrabbling sound. But before she could speak, the kitchen light went out!

"I knew it!" exclaimed Trina. "There's a poltergeist in this house, Cam!"

"A polter-what?" asked Cam, fumbling in the kitchen cupboard for a new lightbulb. "The kitchen light just burned out, that's all."

"A poltergeist!" Trina said the word slowly. "Pol-ter-guy-st! That's a kind of house ghost that plays tricks on people."

"Ouch!" Cam said, burning her fingers on the hot burned-out bulb. "When I get this light fixed, I'll show you who's making that noise. And it's no pol-ter-guy-st!"

When the kitchen light was on again, both girls went into Cam's room. It was full of animals: a cage of crickets, a sleepy kitten, a bowl of goldfish, a glass ant house, and one empty cage with the door hanging open.

"I thought so!" exclaimed Cam. "That bad little hamster has

escaped behind the dresser again! And that's who's making the scrabbling sound!"

"How awful!" said Trina. "Won't the poor little thing get caught back there?"

"No way," Cam answered. "It will come out as soon as it's hungry."

Suddenly Trina looked toward the living room. "Listen!" she said, grabbing Cam's arm. "Do you hear anything?"

"NOW what should I hear?" asked Cam.

"You SHOULD hear the radio!" said Trina. "But someone — or something — has turned it off!"

The girls rushed to the living room and stared at the silent radio.

"WE didn't turn it off," said Cam. "So who did?"

"The poltergeist, of course," said Trina.

Suddenly the front door opened and Cam's sister came in. "What are you two staring at?" she asked.

"Somebody turned off the radio, and it wasn't us!" said Cam. "Trina thinks it's a poltergeist!"

Cam's sister laughed. Then she stamped her foot and the radio began to play.

"Just a loose wire in the radio," she said. "Sorry, there is no poltergeist here."

"Maybe," said Trina. "And maybe not. If there is no poltergeist, then why did the kitchen light burn out, the hamster run behind the dresser, and the radio go off — ALL AT THE SAME TIME?"

Cam and her sister looked at each other. But they couldn't think of an answer.

 ● Answer these questions on your activity paper.

1. What sentence or sentences at the beginning of the story made you wonder what was going to happen in the story?

2. Do you think there was a poltergeist in Cam's house? Why or why not?

3. Do you think the story really happened? Why or why not?

Talking Together

A. Discuss with your classmates the answers you wrote on your activity paper.

B. Is "The Poltergeist" a good title for the story? Why is it important for a story to have an interesting title?

C. Stories can end in different ways. Some story endings are funny, some are exciting, or some can be a surprise. Was the ending of this story funny, exciting, or surprising?

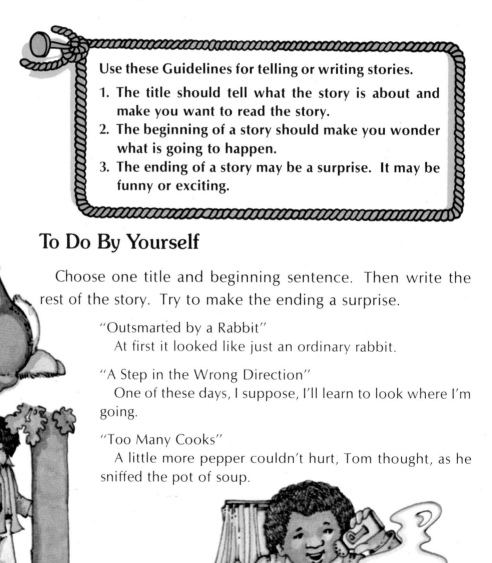

Use these Guidelines for telling or writing stories.

1. **The title should tell what the story is about and make you want to read the story.**
2. **The beginning of a story should make you wonder what is going to happen.**
3. **The ending of a story may be a surprise. It may be funny or exciting.**

To Do By Yourself

Choose one title and beginning sentence. Then write the rest of the story. Try to make the ending a surprise.

"Outsmarted by a Rabbit"
At first it looked like just an ordinary rabbit.

"A Step in the Wrong Direction"
One of these days, I suppose, I'll learn to look where I'm going.

"Too Many Cooks"
A little more pepper couldn't hurt, Tom thought, as he sniffed the pot of soup.

2 Making Stories Interesting

To Read and Think Over

One way to make a story interesting is to tell the exact words people in the story say to each other.

When you write the exact words that a person said, you are writing a **direct quotation.** To show the exact words the person is saying, you must use special punctuation marks called **quotation marks.** Study this example.

"Listen! What's that creaking noise?" whispered Trina.

● Look at "The Poltergeist" on pages 182–183 to answer these questions. Copy the exact quotations on your activity paper. Be sure to include all punctuation marks.

1. What did Trina yell when the kitchen light went out?
2. What did Cam answer when Trina asked about the hamster escaping behind the dresser?
3. What did Cam's sister ask Cam and Trina when she came home?

Talking Together

A. Discuss the direct quotations you wrote on your paper.

B. Where are capital letters used in the direct quotations? Is the punctuation mark at the end of each direct quotation before or after the quotation mark?

C. Look at the story on page 182 again. What happens when one person stops speaking and someone else starts speaking?

Use these Guidelines for writing direct quotations.

1. **Use a direct quotation to show exactly what someone says.**
2. **Begin the first word of each direct quotation with a capital letter.**
3. **Put one pair of quotation marks before the first word of the direct quotation. Put the second pair of quotation marks after the last word and the final punctuation mark of the direct quotation.**
4. **When you are writing direct quotations, begin a new line every time another person speaks. Indent each new line.**

To Do By Yourself

Look at this cartoon. The exact words of the speakers are shown above their heads. Write a paragraph that tells what is happening in the cartoon. Use direct quotations to show each speaker's exact words. Follow the GUIDELINES for writing the direct quotations.

3 Planning and Writing a Story

To Read and Think Over

Now you are ready to write your own story. You may want to write about something that happened to you. It could be something funny, such as trying to learn to ice-skate. It could be something scary, such as some strange noise you heard at night. It might be about something exciting, such as your first sailboat ride.

 ● Copy and complete this chart on your activity paper.

STORY-PLANNING CHART		
WHAT HAPPENED?	TO WHOM DID IT HAPPEN?	HOW DID IT HAPPEN?
List something that happened to you, or something you did that would make an interesting story.	List the people, animals or things that were part of the happening or event.	List as many details as you can about the event.

Study the pictures in this lesson. Think of something that has happened to you. Then answer these questions on your activity paper. You will use your answers later in this lesson.

1. What happened first? Second?
2. How did it turn out?

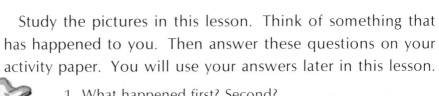

Talking Together

A. Discuss with your classmates the story events you wrote on your paper. Don't tell your classmates the whole story!

B. Read the GUIDELINES for this lesson. If you do not understand them, ask your teacher to explain.

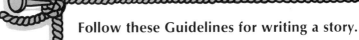

Follow these Guidelines for writing a story.

1. **In the beginning of the story tell something that will make the reader wonder what is going to happen.**
2. **Tell things in the order in which they happened.**
3. **Use direct quotations to make your story more interesting.**
4. **Lead up to a surprise at the end of the story.**
5. **Choose a title that will catch the reader's interest.**

To Do By Yourself

Use the information you listed on your activity paper and write your story. As you write your story, keep the GUIDE-LINES of this lesson in mind. When you have finished your story, proofread it. Copy it on a clean paper if necessary.

4 Talking About Poems

To Read and Think Over

Listen as your teacher reads each of these poems. Then read the poems to yourself.

SOMERSAULTS
& HEADSTANDS

Kathleen Fraser

What are you doing?
  I'm turning a somersault.
How do you do it?
  I put my head in the grass
  and roll over like a snail.
Could you turn a wintersault?
  No, because my head would
  get cold in the snow.

Now, what are you doing?
  A headstand.
Is it like a somersault?
  Well, sort of, but you stop
  in the middle.
How do you keep from falling?
  I pretend everyone else
  is walking upside down.

City

Langston Hughes

In the morning the city
Spreads its wings
Making a song
In stone that sings.

In the evening the city
Goes to bed
Hanging lights
About its head.

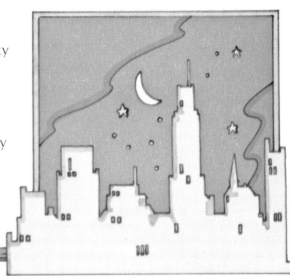

CENTRAL PARK TOURNEY

Mildred Weston

Cars
In the Park
With long spear lights
Ride at each other
Like armored knights;
Rush,
Miss the mark,
Pierce the dark,
Dash by!
Another two
Try.

Staged
In the Park
From dusk
To dawn,
The tourney goes on:
Rush,
Miss the mark,
Pierce the dark,
Dash by!
Another two
Try.

"Central Park Tourney," reprinted by permission; © 1953, The New Yorker Magazine, Inc.

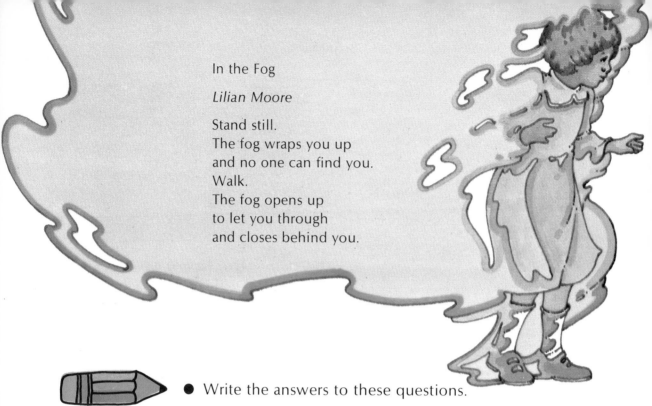

In the Fog

Lilian Moore

Stand still.
The fog wraps you up
and no one can find you.
Walk.
The fog opens up
to let you through
and closes behind you.

● Write the answers to these questions.

1. Which poem do you like best?
2. Why did you like that poem?

Talking Together

A. Discuss with your classmates the answers on your activity paper.

B. Which poem is funny? Which poems describe something? What do they describe?

C. Many poems are divided into sections. A section in a poem is called a **stanza.** "Central Park Tourney" has two stanzas. Where does the second stanza begin?

D. Many poems have **rhyme.** Sometimes each line rhymes with the line above it. Sometimes a second line rhymes with a fourth line. Look at the poem "City." Which lines rhyme?

To Do By Yourself

Copy a poem that you enjoy from a book or a magazine. Be sure to use a capital letter wherever one is used in the poem.

5 Using What You Have Learned

A. Think of an interesting title for each of these story ideas. Write the titles on your paper. Begin the first word, the last word, and all the important words of each title with a capital letter. Review the GUIDELINES on page 184.

1. A story about a day when you woke up grouchy, and everything seemed to go wrong. You lost things, forgot things, and broke things. Then a surprise package arrived for you. The world looked different.

2. A story about the first time you traveled some place by yourself — to school, to the store, downtown, to a friend's or relative's home. You were a little afraid and worried about getting there without help. You did, though, and you didn't get lost.

B. Rewrite each of the sentences. Add quotation marks where they are needed. Review the GUIDELINES on page 186 for writing quotations.

1. Pauline asked, May I take this book out of the library?
2. You may take several books, said the librarian.
3. We're going now, her mother said.
4. But I need more time, protested Pauline.
5. Her mother answered, You may have five more minutes.

WORDS ARE INTERESTING

Alphonso's Photos

Alphonso is proud of his scrapbook. He has written a label under each picture. The label tells who is in the picture and what they are doing. Alphonso wants to add another label. He wants to find a word that tells how the action in each picture was done. You can help him.

1. Number your paper from 1 to 6. Study each picture. Decide how the action is being done. Then choose the word from the "How" Bank that describes the action exactly. (You may use a dictionary to help you.) Write the words on your paper.
2. Look at the words in the "How" Bank again. There are six words you did not use to describe Alphonso's pictures. Write a sentence of your own for each of these words.

The "How" Bank

roughly	noisily	carefully
fairly	fast	secretly
gently	sleepily	busily
happily	gracefully	dangerously

194

Aunt Becky and Todd smiling

①

Sandy running

②

Great-Grandma rocking

③

My sister Martha dancing

④

Mom working

⑤

Dad working

⑥

6 Combining Subjects

To Read and Think Over

Sometimes you may want to combine two short sentences into one longer sentence. Here is one way to do it. Study these sentences. How are the first two combined to make the third sentence?

1. Jane ate popcorn.   2. I ate popcorn.
3. Jane and I ate popcorn.

● Combine these pairs of sentences. Write the new sentences on your activity paper. Be sure to begin and end each sentence correctly.

1. Marvin watched TV.
   I watched TV.

2. Martha wrote us a letter.
   Lee wrote us a letter.

3. Steve liked that book.
   I liked that book.

Talking Together

A. Discuss the sentences you wrote on your paper.

B. Look at the three sentences in *To Read and Think Over.* What are the subjects of sentences 1 and 2? What word is used to combine the subjects in sentence 3?

C. What is the predicate in sentence 3? Is it the same as the predicates of sentences 1 and 2?

D. Make up three sentences for the cartoon at the beginning of the lesson. The first sentence should have one subject. The second sentence should have another subject. The third sentence should have a combined subject.

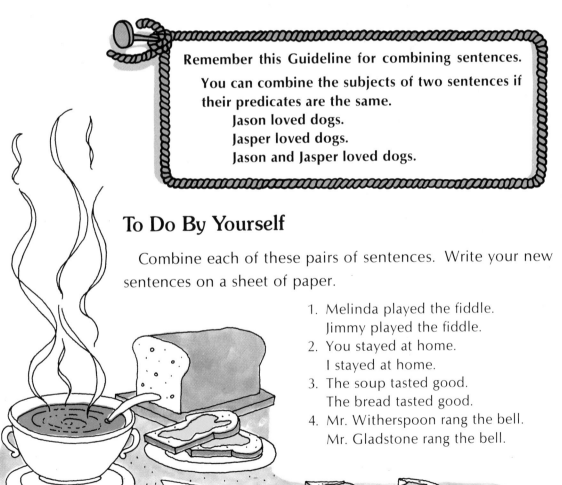

Remember this Guideline for combining sentences.

You can combine the subjects of two sentences if their predicates are the same.
Jason loved dogs.
Jasper loved dogs.
Jason and Jasper loved dogs.

To Do By Yourself

Combine each of these pairs of sentences. Write your new sentences on a sheet of paper.

1. Melinda played the fiddle.
   Jimmy played the fiddle.
2. You stayed at home.
   I stayed at home.
3. The soup tasted good.
   The bread tasted good.
4. Mr. Witherspoon rang the bell.
   Mr. Gladstone rang the bell.

7 Combining Predicates

To Read and Think Over

Study the first two sentences. How are they combined in the third sentence?

1. Hubert ate his sandwich.   2. Hubert drank his milk.
3. Hubert ate his sandwich and drank his milk.

● Combine these pairs of sentences. Write the new sentences on your activity paper. Be sure to begin and end each sentence correctly.

1. I washed my face.
   I brushed my hair.

2. Stella went fishing.
   Stella caught two trout.

3. Mario ran down field.
   Mario caught the ball.

Talking Together

A. Discuss the sentences you wrote on your activity paper.

B. Look at the three sentences in *To Read and Think Over.* What is the predicate in each sentence? What word is used to combine the predicates in sentence 3.

C. Is the subject of each sentence the same or different?

D. Make up three sentences for the cartoon at the beginning of the lesson. The first sentence should have one predicate. The second sentence should have another predicate. The third sentence should have a combined predicate.

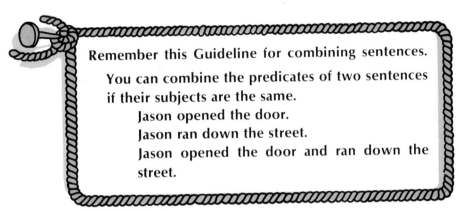

Remember this Guideline for combining sentences.

You can combine the predicates of two sentences if their subjects are the same.
    Jason opened the door.
    Jason ran down the street.
    Jason opened the door and ran down the street.

To Do By Yourself

Combine each of these pairs of sentences. Write the new sentences on your paper.

1. Terence closed the envelope.
   Terence licked the stamp.
2. They left Buffalo.
   They moved to Niagara Falls.
3. The cat washed its face.
   The cat cleaned its paws.
4. Maura raised her hand.
   Maura answered the question.
5. The flower withered.
   The flower died.

199

8 Combining Ideas

To Read and Think Over

Phyllis has too many bags to carry.
How can she carry all her groceries in one trip?

Look at the beginnings of these two stories. Read them both to see which one is more interesting.

1.

One morning I woke up. I woke up early. It was a beautiful day. It was sunny. It was warm. This was a special day. I knew that right away. Something good was going to happen. I went into the kitchen for breakfast. I could smell toast burning. The kitchen was filled with smoke. "That was the last piece of bread," said my brother. "We're out of milk," he said. What kind of day is this, I thought. And it was just beginning!

2.

I woke up early one morning. It was a beautiful day, warm and sunny. I knew right away that this was a special day. Something good was going to happen. As I went into the kitchen for breakfast, I could smell toast burning. The kitchen was filled with smoke. "That was the last piece of bread," said my brother, "and we're out of milk." What kind of special day is this, I thought. And it was just beginning!

200

 ● On your activity paper answer these questions.

1. Which selection do you think is more interesting?

2. In selection 2 what has the author done with the first two sentences of selection 1?

Talking Together

A. Which selection is more interesting? Why?

B. Compare selections 1 and 2. Which one has more sentences? Which one has longer sentences? How have short sentences been combined to make longer sentences?

C. What are some other ways you could combine some of the sentences in the first selection?

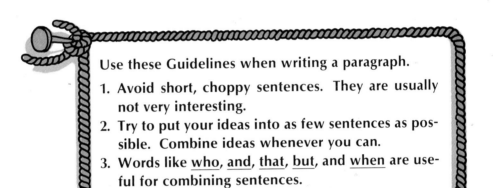

Use these Guidelines when writing a paragraph.

1. Avoid short, choppy sentences. They are usually not very interesting.
2. Try to put your ideas into as few sentences as possible. Combine ideas whenever you can.
3. Words like <u>who</u>, <u>and</u>, <u>that</u>, <u>but</u>, and <u>when</u> are useful for combining sentences.

To Do By Yourself

Combine the ideas in each group of sentences to make one sentence. Write your sentences on your paper.

1. We looked for Jeffrey. We looked in the basement.
2. Vince called Jeffrey's name. Jeffrey didn't answer.
3. I could hear the dog. It was the tan dog. It was barking all night.

4. Shelley made a sandwich. It was a peanut butter sandwich. She made it for lunch.
5. Clara opened the door. She saw something. It made her laugh.

9 Avoiding Unnecessary Words

To Read and Think Over

Some words don't add anything to a story. If you use a great many unnecessary words, your story becomes less interesting. Read this story to see if the underlined words are needed.

The Dog Next Door

Well, have you ever known a dog that was afraid of everything? Well, I have. Why, the dog that lives next door is scared of even a squirrel. When the dog sees the squirrel, the squirrel dashes up a tree. Then the dog runs to the tree and stands there barking. And so, finally the squirrel comes down. Well, when he gets close to the bottom, the dog turns and runs home.

 ● On your activity paper follow these directions.

1. List the words that are underlined in "The Dog Next Door."

2. Tell where in the sentence the underlined words are found.

Talking Together

A. What are the underlined words in the story? What, if anything, does each one tell you?

B. Read "The Dog Next Door" aloud. Then read it aloud again leaving out the underlined words. Did the story sound better the first time or the second time? Why?

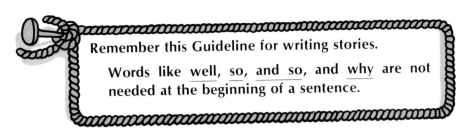

Remember this Guideline for writing stories.

Words like **well**, **so**, and **so**, and **why** are not
needed at the beginning of a sentence.

To Do By Yourself

Rewrite this story on your paper. Take out all the unnecessary words at the beginning of sentences. Be sure to begin and end each sentence correctly.

A Spotted Dog Story

Well, I had always wanted a dog. Why, I even knew what kind of dog I wanted — a Dalmatian. So, I had been promised a dog for my birthday. "It can't be a Dalmatian, though," my parents said. "We can't afford to buy one." Well, I was very disappointed. So, when we went to the Animal Shelter to pick out a dog, I didn't even want to go inside. Well, I was sitting in the car feeling very unhappy when my parents came out with a puppy. Why, it was a fat, black-and-white spotted puppy that ran right over to me and jumped into my arms. Well, I couldn't say no — especially when it was licking my face. Why, I forgot all about Dalmatians that minute. So from then on, my puppy was the only dog I ever wanted.

10 Using What You Have Learned

A. Combine some of these sentences by joining the subjects. Combine the others by joining the predicates. The GUIDE-LINES on pages 197 and 199 may help you.

1. Marlene wrote a story for the school newspaper.
   Leon wrote a story for the school newspaper.
2. Kim read it.
   Kim wrote a letter to the editor.

3. The editor liked her letter.
   The editor printed it.
4. Phyllis saw Kim's letter to the editor.
   I saw Kim's letter to the editor.
5. The letter answered one question.
   The letter asked another question.

B. Rewrite this paragraph. Combine ideas to make smoother sentences. Review the GUIDELINES on page 201.

> Last weekend Luci and I decided to build a tree house. We decided to build it in my backyard. We began work right after breakfast. We worked all day. We finished the tree house. We decided to eat supper in the tree house that night. We went to get tuna sandwiches. We also got some cookies. We had made the cookies the day before.

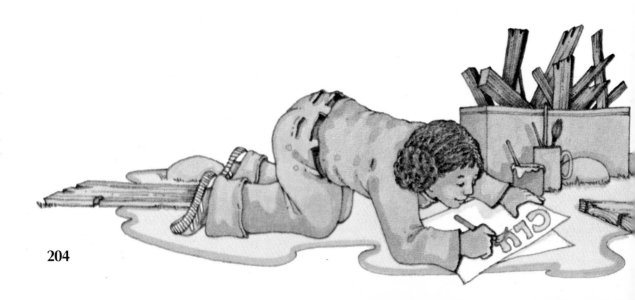

C. Copy this paragraph on your paper. Leave out the words that are not needed at the beginning of some sentences. The GUIDELINE on page 203 may help you.

So, when we got settled in the tree house, we realized that we had forgotten a flashlight. Why, Luci wanted me to go right back down and get one. Well, I didn't want to, and she didn't either. So, finally we decided we didn't need one. Well, by then it was late, and we were almost asleep.

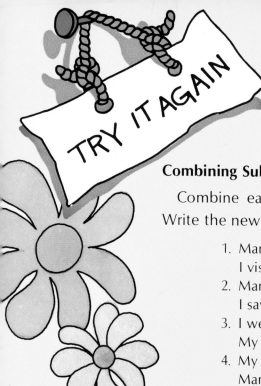

TRY IT AGAIN

Combining Subjects (pages 196–197)

Combine each pair of sentences by joining the subjects. Write the new sentence on your paper.

1. Maria visited Boston.
   I visited Boston.
2. Mary saw a ship, the *Constitution*.
   I saw a ship, the *Constitution*.
3. I went to the science museum.
   My brother went to the science museum.
4. My brother liked the planetarium.
   Maria liked the planetarium.
5. Maria thought we had seen many interesting things.
   I thought we had seen many interesting things.

Combining Predicates (pages 198–199)

Combine each pair of sentences by joining the predicates. Write the new sentence on your paper.

1. Mother took us for a ride on a trolley car.
   Mother showed us the Museum of Fine Arts.
2. We climbed Bunker Hill Monument.
   We took some pictures.
3. We went to the park.
   We ate a picnic lunch.
4. My brother went to the ball game.
   My brother cheered for the home team.
5. Maria went shopping at a big department store.
   Maria bought presents for everyone.

Combining Ideas (pages 200–201)

Combine the short sentences to make longer, more interesting ones. Write the paragraph on your paper.

Last Saturday the girls and boys in our neighborhood had a picnic at the big park. It is in the west end of town. We got to the park late in the morning. We stayed there until the middle of the afternoon. The boys got lunch ready. They cleaned up the tables after we had eaten. Then we pitched horseshoes and played softball. Sally played on one side in the ball game. So did Ann. Sally caught two flies. She also hit a home run. That won the game.

Avoiding Unnecessary Words (pages 202–203)

Copy this paragraph on your paper. Leave out the words that are not needed at the beginnings of some sentences.

Well, the woman who lives next door to us has a dog that is more easily scared than any dog I ever saw. Why, he is scared of even a squirrel. So, for the last month a squirrel has been making a fool of him. Why, the squirrel goes near the dog and then, when the dog sees him, dashes up a tree. Well, the dog runs to the tree and stands there barking for as much as a half hour. So, finally the squirrel starts to chatter and comes down. Well, when he gets close to the bottom, the dog just turns and runs to the front door of the house.

DO YOU REMEMBER ?

Using Personal Pronouns (pages 158–160)

Use a personal pronoun in place of the underlined words in this story. Write the story on your paper.

Coming out of school today, <u>Barbara, Jim, and I</u> saw a man on the sidewalk with a monkey. It was running in circles around <u>the man</u> and chattering. We laughed so loud that I think we frightened <u>the monkey</u>. The monkey started to run away from <u>Barbara, Jim, and me</u>. The man chased after the monkey and finally caught <u>the monkey</u>. <u>The man and the monkey</u> went on down the street.

Using Correct Word Forms (pages 161–163)

Copy these sentences, using the correct words in parentheses.

1. (Lois and I, Lois and me) decided to make animals out of snow.
2. Bill came along and asked (Lois and I, Lois and me) if he could join us.
3. Bill asked (Lois and I, Lois and me) for ideas.
4. (Lois and I, Lois and me) suggested making a leopard, using stones for spots.
5. Then Bill told (Lois and I, Lois and me) that he had an idea.
6. He told (Lois and I, Lois and me) to lie on our backs in the snow and slide our arms back and forth.
7. Then he warned (Lois and I, Lois and me) to get up very carefully.
8. (Lois and I, Lois and me) found we had made angels in the snow.

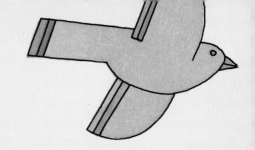

Verbs and Their Tenses (pages 124–128)

Copy these sentences. Change the time in each sentence from present to past by changing the tense of the verb.

1. Don and Pat enjoy picnics.
2. They travel to the park.
3. They pack cookies and two cans of juice.
4. They watch the ducks swimming on the lake.
5. They are ready to go home after two hours.

Subject and Verb Agreement (pages 170–171)

Copy these sentences. Use the verb that agrees with the subject.

1. Dad (bake, bakes) delicious brownies.
2. The ducks (swim, swims) in the pond.
3. You (feed, feeds) the ducks stale bread.
4. Amy (like, likes) to watch them.
5. One duck (walk, walks) to Amy.

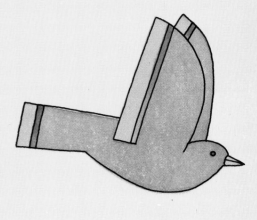

On Your Own

1. You had been wishing very hard for something exciting to happen. Last night, when you opened a book to read, a puff of smoke came out. You heard a strange song. You knew your wish was about to happen. Was it really exciting? Write a story about what happened. The questions may help you.

   What was in the book?
   What did it do?
   What happened?

2. Write a story of your own. If you wish, use one of these sentences to begin your story:

   The day I found the magic boots was a lucky day for me.

   After having been underwater in a submarine for three weeks, we surfaced in a strange, wonderful place.

   As I stood on the colorful rug, it lifted me up in the air, and I flew straight out the window.

3. Did you ever imagine a new kind of animal? Perhaps it was a kitten that had zebra stripes. Write a poem or a story about an unusual animal that is only in *your* head.

   You might want to start your poem like this:

   The (animal) I see in my dreams has a neck like a _____.

4. Spring is just around the corner. How do you know? What do you see? What can you smell? What do you hear?

   Write a poem or a story telling how you know spring is coming? The questions above may help you.

211

FRIENDLY LETTERS

Friendly letters are fun to send and to receive. Who would like a cheerful greeting from you? Write a letter. Tell about interesting things that have happened. Make the other person happy. You'll be happy you did.

1 Writing Friendly Letters

To Read and Think Over

Terence and Kenneth visited their grandparents in Texas. They both wrote a letter home to their older brother Willis. Which letter do you think Willis liked better?

Dear Willis,

    We've been having a great time with Grandma and Grandpa. Do you remember that you wanted a picture of their basset hound's new puppies? Here's a snapshot of them. Grandma and Grandpa really liked the names you suggested for the puppies. In only another week we'll be home. I'll see you then!

Your brother,
Kenneth

Dear Willis,

    We've been at Grandma's and Grandpa's a week. They are okay. Their dog had puppies. We're going to be here another week. I don't know what we are going to do while we're here. I'm not doing much right now. I'll see you in a week.

Your brother,
Terence

● Which letter do you think is more interesting? On your activity paper copy these sentences and fill in the spaces.

I like _____ letter better. I think it is more interesting because _____.

Talking Together

A. Discuss with your classmates the sentences you wrote on your activity paper.

B. What topics would you choose if you were writing a letter to a friend? What has happened to you this week? What interesting things have you seen or done?

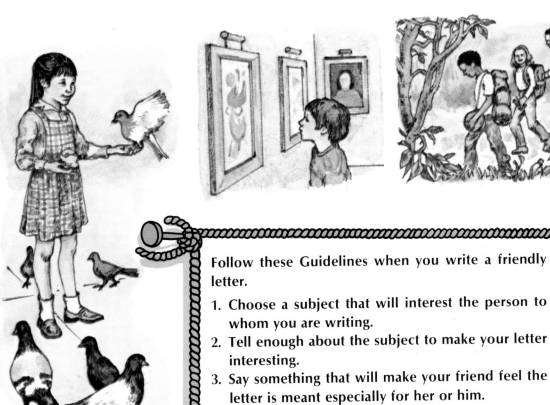

Follow these Guidelines when you write a friendly letter.

1. Choose a subject that will interest the person to whom you are writing.
2. Tell enough about the subject to make your letter interesting.
3. Say something that will make your friend feel the letter is meant especially for her or him.

To Do By Yourself

Think of something you did or that happened to you recently. Which friend of yours might like to hear about it? Write a letter to your friend. Follow the GUIDELINES to make your letter interesting. Remember that writing a friendly letter is like talking to a friend.

2 Learning About the Parts of a Letter

To Read and Think Over

Read this letter carefully. Then read the names of the five parts of the letter and what each part does.

The **Heading** gives the address of the writer and the date.

The **Greeting** is a way of saying hello.

The **Body** is the main part of the letter.

The **Closing** is a way of saying good-by.

The **Signature** is the writer's name.

> 5827 North Tyler Street
> Chicago, Illinois 60660
> March 15, 19 —
>
> Dear Lily,
>   I'm really sorry you won't be able to take part in the school swimming meet. Everyone on the team is sorry that you are sick and won't be able to be here. Take care of yourself and we'll let you know how we do.
>   Your teammate,
>   Rosalie

Read the envelope Rosalie addressed to Lily. Study the two addresses.

The **Return Address** tells who sent the letter.

The **Main Address** tells to whom the letter is being sent.

> Ms. Rosalie Bemis
> 5827 North Tyler Street
> Chicago, Illinois 60660
>
>   Ms. Lily Choy
>   5742 Kenmore Avenue
>   Chicago, Illinois 60660

 ● Copy each sentence on your activity paper. Complete it with the name of one of the parts of a friendly letter or the name of one of the addresses on an envelope.

1. The _____ in a letter gives the writer's address.
2. The _____ is the main part of the letter.
3. The _____ is the part of the letter where the writer says hello.
4. The _____ is the writer's name.
5. In the _____ the writer says good-by.
6. The _____ on the envelope tells to whom the letter is being sent.
7. The _____ on the envelope tells who sent the letter.

Talking Together

A. Discuss the sentences you wrote on your activity paper.

B. Where is each part of the letter placed? Study and discuss the use of capital letters and commas in the model letter. Notice that you must begin the first word in both the greeting and the closing with a capital letter. Commas are used at the end of the greeting and the closing. Study the use of capital letters in the heading. Notice that a comma separates the city from the name of the state. Where is a comma used in the date?

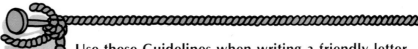

Use these Guidelines when writing a friendly letter.

1. Include all five parts of a friendly letter:
   Heading   Greeting   Body   Closing   Signature
2. Make sure the parts are placed correctly, according to the model letter in this lesson.
3. Use capital letters and punctuation correctly, according to the model letter in this lesson.

To Do By Yourself

Use the body of this letter. Add your own heading, greeting, closing, and signature. Write the letter to a friend.

Last week I went to the museum with my brother. We saw an exhibit called "Transportation Through the Ages." It was really interesting. I'd like to go again. It would be fun if we could go together sometime.

Then draw an envelope and address it to your friend. Be sure to proofread your work.

3 Thank-You Letters

To Read and Think Over

Simon took care of Jeffrey's pet while Jeffrey was away with his family. Read the thank-you letter Jeffrey wrote. If you were Simon, would you like receiving this letter?

9 Oak Street
Medicine Hat, Alberta
T1A 7E6
July 20, 19—

Dear Simon,

Thank you for taking care of Rufus these last two weeks. I felt a lot better about leaving him once I knew he could stay with you. When I came over to get him yesterday, Rufus looked happy and healthy. Thanks again from Rufus and me.

Your friend,
Jeffrey

● Write the answers to these questions on your activity paper.

1. How soon did Jeffrey write the thank-you letter?
2. What sentence tells how the favor helped Jeffrey?
3. Which sentences say thank you?
4. What sentence says that Jeffrey was pleased?

219

Talking Together

A. Discuss with your classmates the answers you wrote on your activity paper. Do you think Simon liked receiving this letter? Why or why not?

B. What are some other reasons for writing thank-you letters? Has someone done you or your class a favor? Has someone sent you a gift?

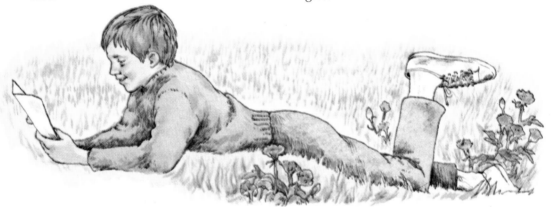

Follow these Guidelines when you write a thank-you letter.

1. Write a thank-you letter soon after you have received a gift or soon after someone has done you a favor.
2. Tell how you have used or will use the gift, or how the favor has helped you.
3. Say something to show that you are pleased by the other person's thoughtfulness.

To Do By Yourself

Write a thank-you letter to someone who has sent you a gift or done you a favor. Be sure to include all the parts of a letter and to place them correctly.

4 Writing Invitations

To Read and Think Over

The fourth-grade class is having a party. The pupils wrote this letter inviting Mr. Garland's class to join them. What information did they put in their invitation?

Dear Mr. Garland and Members of the Fifth Grade,

    We are having a party to celebrate the last day of school. There will be refreshments. Could you join us in our classroom on Thursday, June 23, at 1:30?
    We are looking forward to showing you the posters we made. We hope you can be there.

Your friends,
Mrs. Reeves and the
Fourth-Grade Class

 ● Answer these questions on your activity paper.

1. In the letter which sentence tells the purpose of the invitation?
2. On what date and at what time of day is the party?
3. Where is the party going to be held?
4. Which sentence says that the fourth-grade class really wants the fifth-grade class to come to the party?

Talking Together

A. Discuss with your classmates the answers you wrote on your activity paper.

B. Discuss with your classmates how to write a reply to an invitation. Help your classmates write one letter accepting the invitation from the fourth grade and one letter refusing it.

> Follow these Guidelines when you write an invitation.
>
> 1. Tell what the purpose of the invitation is.
> 2. Tell the date and time when the event will take place.
> 3. Tell where the event will take place.
> 4. Make the person you are inviting feel you want him or her to come.

To Do By Yourself

Choose a partner. Write an invitation to your partner to go to the circus next Saturday. Follow the GUIDELINES for writing an invitation. Proofread your work.

5 Writing Announcements

To Read and Think Over

Sometimes you want many people to know about an event. You need to write an announcement instead of an invitation. Read these three announcements. Which one tells everything you would need to know about the talent show?

A
Come to BIG TALENT UNDER THE BIG TOP —the all-school talent show — May 25, at 3:30. Everyone come and see the singers, dancers, jugglers, and magicians.

B
Everyone come and see the singers, dancers, jugglers, and magicians in the school auditorium on May 25, at 3:30.

C
BIG TALENT UNDER THE BIG TOP — the all-school talent show — will be given by the Gym Club on May 25. Come to the school auditorium at 3:30 and see the singers, dancers, jugglers, and magicians!

● Copy this chart. The boxes are marked A, B, and C to match the announcements on page 223. Place check marks in the proper box to show what each announcement tells.

	A	B	C
Tells **what** the event is			
Tells **where** the event will be held			
Tells **when** the event will be held			
Tells **who** is planning the event			

Talking Together

A. Discuss with your classmates the information you listed on your chart.

B. For which of these events would you write announcements? For which would you write invitations?

a slumber party   a class play
a garage sale   a museum trip

Follow these Guidelines when you write an announcement.

1. **Tell what event is going to happen.**
2. **Tell when the event is going to happen.**
3. **Tell where the event will take place.**
4. **Tell who is planning the event.**

To Do By Yourself

Write an announcement for a school bake sale that your class will hold in your school gym on Friday. Be sure to follow the GUIDELINES and to include all the information anyone would need to know.

6 Using What You Have Learned

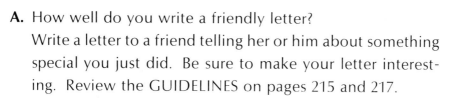

A. How well do you write a friendly letter?
Write a letter to a friend telling her or him about something special you just did. Be sure to make your letter interesting. Review the GUIDELINES on pages 215 and 217.

B. How well do you know the parts of a letter?
List the five parts of a friendly letter. Then write a sentence or two that explains what each part does. Review the GUIDELINES on page 217.

C. How well do you write thank-you letters?
Someone has just given you two tickets to a baseball game. Write a thank-you letter. Use the GUIDELINES on page 220 to help you.

D. How well do you write invitations?
Write a letter inviting a friend to spend a week at your house. Review the GUIDELINES on page 222.

E. How well do you write announcements?
Read this announcement. What facts are missing? Review the GUIDELINES on page 224. Then rewrite the announcement. Add the facts needed to make it complete.

Come Fly a Kite!

Bring your kite to the all-day Kite Fly-In, sponsored by the City-wide Kite Club. Prizes will be given, and refreshments will be sold.

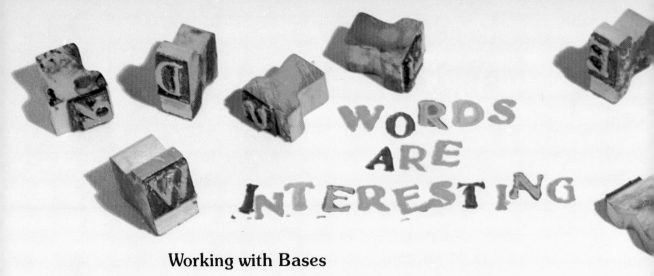

WORDS ARE INTERESTING

Working with Bases

Here are some pictures of Ms. Teachright's classroom. Look at the words under the pictures. Find the part of each word that is the same. This part is called the **base word.**

When you add a word part to a base word, you can make another word. What word parts have been added to the word *order* under each picture?

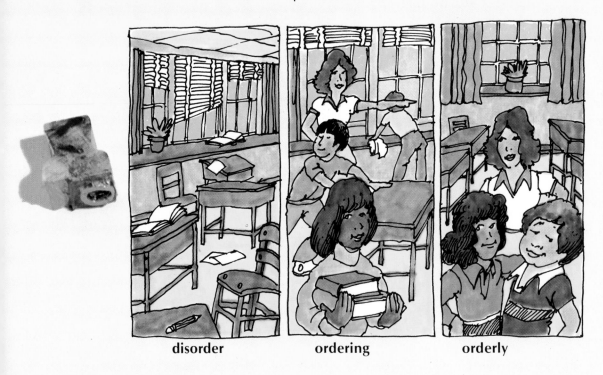

| disorder | ordering | orderly |

226

After Ms. Teachright's room had been picked up, everyone played a word game called *Word Forest*. You can play it, too. Here's how:

1. On your paper draw a tree trunk for each base word listed below. Make each tree grow by adding parts to each base word. For each new word you form, draw a branch. Write the word on the branch. Look at the tree in the picture.

2. Try these word parts at the beginnings of base words:

   un-   re-   dis-

   Try these word parts at the ends of base words:

-ly	**-ful**	**-ing**
-ness		**-less**

3. Check the dictionary to make sure your new words are real words. Check spelling in the dictionary, too. Give yourself one point for each correct word you make.

   Base Words

care	fear	color
appear	arm	rest
do	like	help

7 Learning About Commas in a Letter

To Read and Think Over

Have you learned where commas are used in the heading, greeting, and closing of a letter? Study the parts of this letter. Notice the ways the commas are used.

33 Old Orchard Street
Prince George, British Columbia
V2L   4V3
February 7, 19_____

Dear Sandra,

A group of us went on a bicycle trip. We rode fifteen miles and ended up at Jack's house. We had a really nice picnic. Maybe we can plan to take a long bicycle ride when you visit. You can use my sister's bicycle.

Your cousin,
Louise

Copy the sentences on page 229 on your activity paper. Write the word that best fits each space in the sentence. Choose from these four words or phrases.

day   after   state or province   year

1. In the heading of a letter, a comma is used between the name of the city or town and the _____.
2. A comma is also used in the heading between the _____ and the _____.
3. Commas are used _____ the greeting and the closing of a letter.

Talking Together

A. Discuss with your classmates the sentences you wrote on your activity paper.

B. Make up a heading, a greeting, and a closing for a letter. Tell where commas are used in each one.

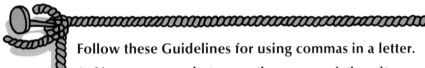

Follow these Guidelines for using commas in a letter.

1. **Use a comma between the name of the city or town and the name of the state.**
2. **Use a comma between the day and the year.**
3. **Use a comma after the greeting of a friendly letter.**
4. **Use a comma after the closing of a friendly letter.**

To Do By Yourself

Copy each heading, greeting, and closing. Add commas where they are needed.

HEADINGS	GREETINGS	CLOSINGS
6824 Audubon Avenue Baton Rouge Louisiana 70816 May 12 19__	Dear Laurie	Your friend Nora
682 Tompkins Street Kansas City Missouri 64132 October 21 19__	Dear Craig	Your cousin Wilma
89 Chestnut Drive Burlington Ontario L7R 3Z2 March 6 19__	Dear Harvey	Your friend Ira

8 Using Commas in a Series

To Read and Think Over

In talking, you pause to make your meaning clear. We call these pauses **juncture.** In writing, you use commas instead of pauses to make your meaning clear. Read this sentence softly to yourself. Listen for juncture. Notice where commas are placed.

Linda bought cheese, tomatoes, soup, and bread.

The sentence above contains a list, or series, of foods. When we say a series of things, we usually pause slightly after each item. Therefore, we place commas after each item in the series.

Now read this sentence. It contains a series, or list, made up of groups of words. Where are the commas used?

We sang songs, read books, rode bikes, and went hiking.

230

Commas are placed after each group of words in the series. Did you notice the word *and* used between the last comma and the last item in the series?

In this sentence, how many people are coming to the party?

> Linda Sue Billy Joe Dora Jane and Earl are coming to the party.

Are seven people coming?

> Linda, Sue, Billy, Joe, Dora, Jane, and Earl are coming to the party.

Or are four people coming?

> Linda Sue, Billy Joe, Dora Jane, and Earl are coming to the party.

Commas help to make your meaning clear.

 ● Copy each sentence twice on your activity paper. First, add commas to make a list of four things. Then add commas to make a list of seven things.

1. Tunafish sandwiches chocolate milk pineapple cake and cookies were on the table.
2. Their interests are riding horses collecting shells painting flowers and singing.
3. Anita Sue Andrew John Mary Teresa and Peter are at the park.

Talking Together

Discuss with your classmates the sentences you wrote on your activity paper.

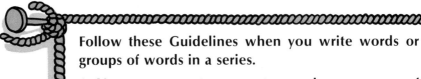

Follow these Guidelines when you write words or groups of words in a series.

1. Use a comma to separate words or groups of words in a series.
2. Use the words <u>and</u> or <u>or</u> between the last comma and the last item in a series.

    I would like bacon, eggs, <u>and</u> toast.
    You can have milk, juice, <u>or</u> water.

To Do By Yourself

Copy these sentences. Add commas to separate the words or groups of words in the series.

1. We planned a picnic for the fourth-grade class the fifth-grade class and the sixth-grade class.
2. The five people in charge of the food are Maria Dean Sophie Lloyd and Philip.
3. They decided to have hot dogs potato chips milk and marshmallows.
4. We invited our teachers parents brothers and sisters.
5. We planned to eat food run races play ball and toast marshmallows.

9 Using Commas with Yes and No

To Read and Think Over

Sentences that answer a question often begin with the words *yes* or *no*. Read each question and its answer. Where is the comma placed in each answer?

Have you lived here long?
No, I just moved here.

Do you know the people next door?
Yes, we met yesterday.

When *yes* or *no* begins a sentence, a comma is used to separate it from the rest of the sentence.

 ● Read each question. Then write a sentence on your activity paper to answer each question. Begin each answer with *yes* or *no*. Be sure to place commas where they are needed.

1. Do you like to swim?
2. Have you ever been on an airplane?
3. Do you have any pets?
4. Do you like birthday parties?
5. Have you ever visited a farm?

Talking Together

A. Discuss with your classmates the sentences you wrote on your activity paper. Where did you place the comma?

B. Make up a question that can be answered with a sentence beginning with *yes* or *no*. Call on a classmate to answer the question. Your classmate should pause after the word *yes* or *no*. This will show where a comma would be placed if the sentence were written.

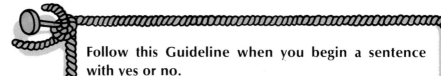

Follow this Guideline when you begin a sentence with <u>yes</u> or <u>no</u>.

Use a comma after the word <u>yes</u> or <u>no</u> when it begins the answer to a question.

To Do By Yourself

Copy these sentences. Add commas where they are needed.

1. No I don't believe you.
2. Yes he really said that.
3. Yes I thought so.
4. No Richard didn't want to ask that.
5. Yes it seemed very strange.
6. No we didn't know anyone.
7. No Rena wasn't there.
8. Yes Angela would be happy to come along.
9. No I haven't seen her yet.
10. Yes our plans are all set.

10 Reviewing Quotation Marks

To Read and Think Over

You know that direct quotations tell the exact words that someone said. You also know how they are written. Study these sentences in which quotations are written correctly.

Michael turned to speak to Tom. "Look how deep the snow is!" he exclaimed. "It will be hard work digging out the walk."

"We may as well begin shoveling," said Tom. He started toward the house and added, "I'll get the shovels."

"Can I help you get them?" asked Michael.

● In this paragraph, each sentence has a direct quotation in it. Write each sentence correctly. Add punctuation marks, capital letters, and quotation marks where they are needed. Use the sentences you have just studied as a model. Be sure to indent the line each time a different person speaks.

Let's go to the park said Nancy shall I bring the ball asked Jean yes that's a good idea answered Nancy everyone else is already there she added okay, I'm ready said Jean

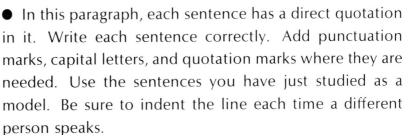

Talking Together

A. Discuss with your classmates the sentences that you wrote on your activity paper.

B. How does the first word of a direct quotation begin? When is a question mark used in a direct quotation? When is an exclamation mark used? How many pairs of quotation marks are used in a direct quotation? Where are they placed?

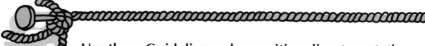

Use these Guidelines when writing direct quotations.

1. **Begin the first word of each direct quotation with a capital letter.**
2. **Put one pair of quotation marks before the first word of the direct quotation. Put the second pair of quotation marks after the last word and the final punctuation mark of the quotation.**
3. **Begin the direct quotation on a new line every time a different person speaks. Indent each of these new lines.**

To Do By Yourself

Copy this story. Follow the GUIDELINES to add capital letters, quotation marks, commas, and other punctuation marks where they are needed.

We turn here said Theo as he rounded the corner. Where are we asked Jane. This doesn't look like Hawes Street. Don't worry answered Theo. I've been here hundreds of times. Jane looked at the map. Then she said the museum should be on our right, but it isn't. I think we've gone the wrong way, Theo.

11 Reviewing Capital Letters

To Read and Think Over

Read this letter. Study the words which begin with capital letters.

7 Hammond Lane
Salt Lake City, Utah
May 16, 19___

Dear Michele,

I have just read an exciting book from my Aunt Ellen. I know you will want to read it. The book is *Stevie and his Seven Orphans* by Miriam E. Mason. The story is about a boy who finds seven puppies and adopts them.

My brother also read the book. He said, "That's the best book I've ever read."

Your friend,
Pauline

 ● Write the body of this letter on your activity paper. Add capital letters where they are needed.

> uncle tim and i were wondering if you could spend your vacation with us in san juan. the other day uncle tim said, we haven't seen susan for a long time.
>
> we have some new neighbors. they have a daughter maria. she is about your age. mr. lopez said, i will take the girls to see the fishing boats in the harbor. when your niece is visiting.
>
> susan, let me know if your vacation starts on april 22.

Talking Together

Discuss the letter you wrote on your activity paper.

Follow these Guidelines for using capital letters.

1. Write the word **I** as a capital letter.
2. Use a capital letter in writing an initial that stands for a name.
3. Use a capital letter to begin:
   a. the first word of a sentence.
   b. a proper noun.
   c. the first word, the last word, and every important word in a group of words that is a proper noun.
   d. the abbreviation for a title.
   e. the first word in both the greeting and the closing of a letter.
   f. the first word, the last word, and each important word in a title.
   g. the first word in a direct quotation.

To Do By Yourself

Pretend you received the letter you wrote on your activity paper. Write a reply either accepting or refusing the invitation.

12 Using What You Have Learned

Practice using commas and direct quotations by correcting this letter. Add commas, quotation marks, and capital letters where they are needed. You will need twenty commas, six pairs of quotation marks, and three capital letters.

8814 Ralston Drive
Lincoln Nebraska 68508
November 2 19___

Dear Beverly

I can hardly wait to tell you about the adventure Cal Eleanor and I had yesterday. Eleanor asked would you like to go on a hike?

I said yes I would like to go.

The weather is really nice said Eleanor. The three of us packed a huge lunch to take along. We took sandwiches hardboiled eggs milk and cookies.

Can you guess what happened? Yes it turned cold and rainy. We had to give up our hike. But we didn't want to give up the picnic.

We can have the picnic in my basement said Cal. We spread a blanket on the floor opened our picnic basket and passed around the eggs.

I asked is there any salt?

No we forgot it said Cal.

So we ate our eggs without salt. We all forgot that we could go upstairs to the kitchen and get some. It was a real picnic after all.

Your friend
Sandra

239

TRY IT AGAIN

Using Commas (pages 228–232)

Copy this invitation. Add commas where they are needed. You will need to add 10 commas.

Dear Girls and Boys

The cooking class the sewing class and the shop class of the River Road School invite you your teachers and your bus drivers to see some of the things we have made. We hope that you can come next Thursday afternoon at two o'clock. Our things will be displayed in Room 4 Room 8 and Room 9. After you see the display, come to Room 22 for cookies lemonade and popcorn balls.

Sincerely yours
Jonah Price

Using Quotation Marks (pages 235–236)

Copy these sentences. Add quotation marks, capital letters, and commas where they are needed. Be sure to add a comma after *yes* or *no*.

1. Susan asked do you have a book about jets?
2. Pamela answered no my brother has one.
3. Tom asked would you like to read the new one I found in the library?
4. Pamela replied yes I would like that very much.
5. Susan asked may I read it when you are finished with it?
6. Pamela said yes I will bring it over to your house next week.
7. Tom asked can I borrow it again to show my cousin Mike?
8. Of course you can Pamela replied.
9. Tom asked have you ever met my cousin?
10. Pamela said no I wasn't here last year during his visit.
11. This movie is going to be exciting said Rosa.
12. Judy suggested we'd better walk faster, or we'll be late.
13. Rosa asked what time does it begin?
14. It starts at two but I can't remember where it is playing answered Judy.
15. Rosa said I don't know where it's playing either.

DO YOU REMEMBER ?

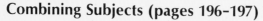

Combining Subjects (pages 196–197)

Combine each pair of sentences by joining the subjects.

1. Gina found a baby squirrel in the woods.
   I found a baby squirrel in the woods.
2. Ann couldn't find its nest.
   Gina couldn't find its nest.
3. Mike thought we should take it home.
   I thought we should take it home.

Combining Predicates (pages 198–199)

Combine each pair of sentences by joining the predicates.

1. The squirrel couldn't open its eyes.
   The squirrel couldn't find its nest.
2. The squirrel was hungry.
   The squirrel shook all over.
3. The squirrel liked warm milk.
   The squirrel enjoyed the nest we made for it.

Using Correct Word Forms (pages 164–168)

A. Copy these sentences. Use <u>good</u> or <u>well</u> in each space.

1. Yesterday I saw a _____ swimming contest.
2. All the swimmers could swim very _____.
3. I do not swim half as _____ as those people.
4. My sister is a _____ swimmer.
5. Some day I hope I swim as _____ as she does.

B. Copy these sentences. Use <u>to</u>, <u>two</u>, or <u>too</u> in each space.

    1. My father brought me some books _____ read.
    2. Today it was _____ cold to go out.
    3. I stayed inside and read _____ books.
    4. My brother decided to read them _____.
    5. We both like _____ read adventure stories.
    6. We still have _____ more books to read.

C. Copy these sentences. Use <u>there</u> or <u>their</u> in each space.

    1. Ned and Barbara brought _____ pet rabbit to school.
    2. _____ was a lot of excitement in our class.
    3. We asked them what they fed _____ pet.
    4. We wondered if _____ was a way to keep it overnight.
    5. All _____ friends wanted to play with the rabbit.

On Your Own

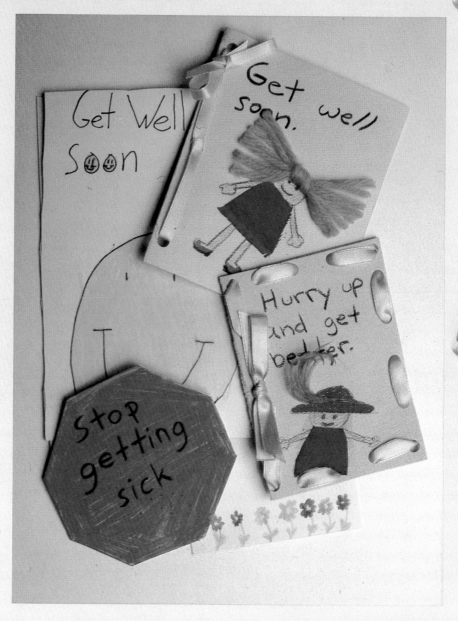

1. One of your friends is sick. Draw a get-well card to send to your friend. Write a verse or greeting to go inside. The card can be fancy, or it can be funny. But be sure it is cheerful.

2. You were climbing a tree in the woods and found this note in a squirrel hole.

Dear New Friend,

I live in the neighborhood and would like to make a new friend. I am 11 years old, like to play baseball and chess, and love to eat pizza. If you would like to be my friend, leave another letter in this hole. Tell me what you like to do and how we can meet.

Your unknown friend,
X

Write an answer to "X" describing yourself, saying what you like to do, and how you can meet.

3. You found a letter someone wrote many years ago in an old chest in the attic. This letter told about some important people and events at that time. Write a letter that you might like someone to read 50 years from now. Tell about a few important people or events. Address your letter to "Dear Future Reader."

4. Write a poem about something that interests you. You may use one of the ideas from this list, or think of your own subject.

a funny animal
a busy street
the smell of something being cooked outdoors
worn-out shoes

8

DESCRIPTIONS

A description helps others see exactly what you see. When you describe something, you ask people to walk in your shoes. You help them see, using only words. Be exact. Tell the difference between what you are describing and something like it. Think of your audience when you describe.

1 Deciding What to Tell

PEARS

PINEAPPLE

AVOCADO

To Read and Think Over

Riddles can be fun to solve. Can you solve this one? "I am thinking of a fruit. It is oval-shaped and has a greenish skin. Can you guess which fruit I am thinking about?"

A good description is not a guessing game. When you describe something well, people do not have to guess what you have in mind.

How can you write a good description? You can study the object you want to describe. Then ask the following questions about it.

1. What is it?
2. What does it look like?
3. What is it used for?

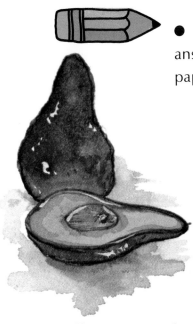

● Read this description of an avocado. Then write the answers to the questions that follow on your activity paper.

An avocado is a fruit that grows on a tree. It is shaped like a pear and is about the size of a softball. It has a leathery, greenish-black skin. Inside is a greenish-yellow pulp which has a bland taste. An avocado has one large seed in the middle. People eat avocado raw, either by itself or in salads.

1. Which underlined word tells what an avocado is?
2. Which underlined words tell what an avocado looks like?
3. Which underlined words tell how it is used?

Talking Together

A. Discuss the answers you wrote on your activity paper.

B. Think of another fruit or a vegetable. With your classmates give a description of it.

Use this Guideline when you give a description.

A good description usually answers these questions.
1. **What is it?**
2. **What does it look like?**
3. **What is it used for?**

To Do By Yourself

A. Look around your classroom. Find something that you can describe. Write a description of it. Answer as many of the GUIDELINE questions as you can.

B. If you are asked to, read your description to your classmates. Have them tell which of the GUIDELINE questions you answered.

2 Telling Enough

To Read and Think Over

Barry saw a picture of a funny creature in a book. He wanted Joan to draw one like it for the bulletin board on *Make-Believe Creatures*. This is the description he gave to Joan. Read it to see if you could draw a picture from Barry's description.

> It was an imaginary creature. Part of its body was fuzzy and part of it was smooth. It was purple with funny eyes. It had some teeth and claws. It had a long tail with fur.

Barry didn't give Joan enough information. She couldn't draw the creature, so Barry wrote the description again. Read how he described it this time.

> It was an imaginary creature. Its head and body were all fuzzy, but its face and tail were smooth. It was a bright purple, with round, popping eyes. It had two fangs, and there were two claws on each of its four paws. Its long tail had a ball of fur on the end.

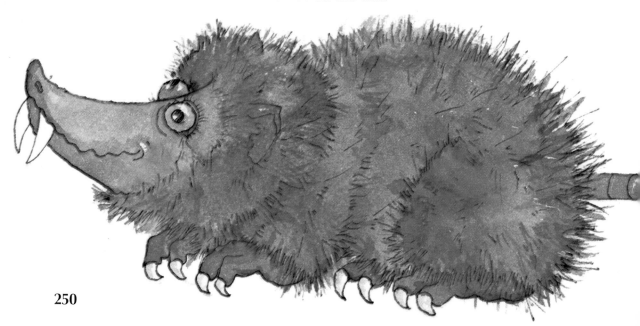

 ● Which words in Barry's second description answer these questions? Write them on your activity paper.

1. Which words tell what is different about this creature's face?
2. Which words tell what is different about this creature's eyes?
3. Which words tell what is different about its teeth?
4. Which words tell what is different about its tail?

Talking Together

A. Discuss with your classmates the answers you wrote on your activity paper.

B. What other things did Barry include, in his second description, that tell how the creature is different from other creatures?

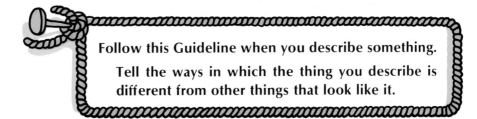

Follow this Guideline when you describe something.

Tell the ways in which the thing you describe is different from other things that look like it.

To Do By Yourself

Write a description of the building you live in. Think about what makes it different from other buildings on your street. Include enough information so that your building would not be mistaken for another building on your street. Proofread your description when you finish writing it.

3 Using Exact Words

To Read and Think Over

Ann and Joe run a sandwich shop. Here is how they describe their roast beef sandwich in a TV ad.

Your teeth will <u>glide</u> silently through the <u>tender</u> <u>brown</u> crust of homemade bread. Then they will <u>crunch</u> and <u>crackle</u> through some <u>crisp</u> <u>green</u> lettuce. Finally, they will meet the <u>tender</u>, <u>juicy</u> goodness of roast beef. The <u>sharp</u> <u>sweet-sour</u> smell of our home-style mustard will make you glad you chose Ann and Joe's Eats to satisfy your lunchtime hunger!

Ann and Joe really want you to try one of their roast beef sandwiches! Look at the underlined words. Ann and Joe are aiming their message at your eyes, ears, nose, and mouth. They tell you how their sandwich looks, sounds, smells, and tastes — and even how it feels to your teeth when you bite into it!

 ● Copy this chart on your activity paper. Then copy the underlined word or words under the heading that tells what Ann and Joe are aiming at.

LOOK	SOUND	SMELL	TASTE	FEEL

Talking Together

A. Compare your chart with the ones your classmates did. Can some words fit under more than one heading? If so, which words are they?

B. Think of some other exact words you would use to describe the way something looks, sounds, smells, tastes, or feels.

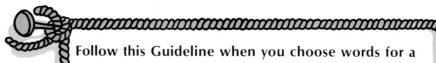

Follow this Guideline when you choose words for a description.

Find words that tell exactly how something looks, sounds, smells, tastes, or feels.

To Do By Yourself

A. Choose something to describe. It can be one of the objects in the pictures on page 253, or it can be something you think of yourself. Think of as many words as you can that tell exactly how the object looks, sounds, smells, tastes, and feels. Make a list of these words. Use as many different kinds of words as you can.

B. Now write a description of the object you chose, using the words from your list.

How does a rabbit smell?   With its nose!

4 Using What You Have Learned

A. How well do you use exact words?

Think of five words that tell something exact for each of these general words.

    1. size   3. shape

    2. color   4. texture

B. How well do you describe things?

Write a description of one of the pictured objects. Try to tell what it is, what it does or how it is used, and what it looks like. Tell enough so that it will not be mistaken for any other object.

WORDS ARE INTERESTING

What's the Word?

Do you eat frankfurters, wieners, or hot dogs? Do you drink soda, pop, or tonic?

Here is a frankfurter.

Here is a frankfurter:

Here is a wiener.

Here is a wiener:

Here is a hot dog.

Here is a hot dog:

They look the same. They taste the same. They ARE the same!

Sometimes, the exact word you need depends on where you are. People use different words for the same thing. But remember — the words are different, not better.

Read this picture story. Then copy the story, writing a word for each picture.

Todd finished his and his dad started washing the Dad turned off the "What's for lunch at school?" Dad asked.

"Sloppy joes and ," Todd answered.

"Do you want to carry lunch?" Dad said. "I can put a sandwich and some 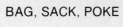 in a for you."

"No, that's O.K.," said Todd. "I like sloppy joes. And they have for dessert."

"All right," said Dad. "Here's your lunch money. Now get your books together. The bus will be here soon."

 FLAPJACKS, PANCAKES, GRIDDLE CAKES

 SPIDER, SKILLET, FRYING PAN

 FAUCET, TAP, SPIGOT

BUTTER BEANS, LIMA BEANS

GOOBERS, GROUND NUTS, PEANUTS

BAG, SACK, POKE

DOUGHNUTS, FRY CAKES

5 Recognizing Adjectives

To Read and Think Over

Read this paragraph to yourself. Pay special attention to the words in blue.

> A **young** fox crawled out of its **dark** den. It wriggled its **black** nose and sniffed the **fresh** air. The **warm** sun felt cozy on the **little** animal's **soft, fluffy** coat.

Did you notice that each word printed in blue adds meaning to the noun that follows? For example, *young* tells or describes *what kind of fox.* A word that is used to describe something or someone is called an **adjective.**

An adjective will complete sentences like these:

The _____ dog chased me.
It is very _____.

 ● Number your activity paper from 1 to 5. Find the adjective in each of these sentences. Write it next to its numeral.

1. An old tree stood in the yard.
2. Its branches were bare.
3. A dead leaf fell from the top.
4. There were holes in the gray bark.
5. A squirrel had built a warm nest.

258

Talking Together

A. Discuss the adjectives you wrote on your activity paper. Find the word in the sentence that each adjective describes.

B. Discuss with your classmates adjectives that describe a food, a television program, or a game.

> **Use these Guidelines to recognize adjectives.**
>
> 1. **A word is an adjective when it is used to describe something or someone.**
> 2. **An adjective will fit into sentences like these.**
>   **The _____ dog chased me.**
>   **It is very _____.**

To Do By Yourself

A. Find the adjectives in these sentences. Write them on your paper.

1. A big horse trotted by.
2. It had a shiny coat.
3. Its tail was long.

4. A small child sat on the gray horse.
5. She held on to the silky mane.

B. Add an adjective to complete each of these sentences. Write the sentences on your paper.

1. The night was _____.
2. A _____ moon was shining.
3. A _____ breeze blew.
4. Two _____ toads hopped by.
5. Everything seemed _____.

C. Use each of these adjectives in a sentence.

heavy   pale   slow   cheerful   smooth

6 Comparing with Adjectives

To Read and Think Over

Look at the picture. Read the sentence under each one. Study the words in color. Did you notice the first sentence says one person is *tall?* The second sentence compares two people. *Taller* is the special form of *tall* used to compare two people. The third sentence compares more than two people. The special form of *tall* used in that sentence is *tallest.*

Stacy is tall. Brian is taller Annmarie is the
               than Stacy.   tallest of all.

Adjectives have special forms to compare two or more people or things. Look again at the words printed in blue. Did you notice the ending -er added to *tall* when two people or things are compared? The ending -est is added to *tall* when more than two people or things are compared.

 ● On your activity paper copy and complete this chart.

ONE	COMPARING TWO	COMPARING MORE THAN TWO
1. small	_____	_____
2. _____	shorter	_____
3. thick	_____	_____
4. _____	_____	warmest
5. cold	_____	_____

Talking Together

A. Discuss the special forms of the adjectives you wrote on the chart. Think of sentences for each of the adjectives. Share your sentences with your classmates.

B. What ending do you add to an adjective when you compare two persons or things? What ending do you add when you compare more than two persons or things?

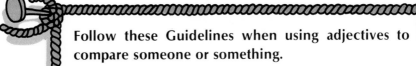

Follow these Guidelines when using adjectives to compare someone or something.

1. The ending -er is added to many adjectives to compare two people or things.
2. The ending -est is added to many adjectives to compare more than two people or things.

To Do By Yourself

A. Rewrite sentences **b** and **c** in each group below. Add the correct form of the adjective used in sentence **a.**

1. a. The yellow book is old.
   b. The green book is _____ than the yellow one.
   c. The red book is the _____ of all.
2. a. Fuzzy has a short tail.
   b. Floppy has a _____ tail than Fuzzy.
   c. Fluffy has the _____ tail of all.
3. a. The table is new.
   b. The chair is the _____ of all.
   c. The lamp is _____ than the table.

4. a. The noodles are hot.
   b. The stew is _____ than the noodles.
   c. The carrots are the _____ of all.
5. a. Carrie's nose is cold.
   b. Her hands are _____ than her nose.
   c. Her feet are the _____ of all.

B. Think of a sentence for each of these adjectives. Write the sentences on your paper. Begin and end them correctly.

1. younger	3. smaller	5. higher
2. youngest	4. smallest	6. highest

7 Special Forms of Adjectives

To Read and Think Over

Many adjectives add the endings _-er_ or _-est_ to compare two or more persons or things. Some adjectives do not have an _-er_ or _-est_ form. Study the adjectives in these sentences.

This is a **bad** storm.
The storm last week was **worse.**
That was the **worst** storm of the winter.

This book has **good** stories.
They are **better** than the stories in the red book.
The **best** stories of all are in the book on the table.

Did you notice that _worse_ and _better_ are used to compare two persons or things? _Worst_ and _best_ are used to compare more than two persons or things.

 ● On your activity paper write six sentences. Use one of these adjectives in each sentence.

good	bad
better	worse
best	worst

Talking Together

A. Share the sentences you wrote with your classmates.

B. Which words are used to compare two people or things?

C. Which words are used to compare more than two people or things?

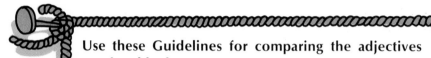

> **Use these Guidelines for comparing the adjectives good and bad.**
>
> **1.** Use <u>better</u> or <u>worse</u> to compare two people or things.
> **2.** Use <u>worst</u> or <u>best</u> to compare more than two people or things.

To Do By Yourself

Add *good, better,* or *best* to each sentence. Copy the sentences on your paper.

1. Apple pie is _____ than the blueberry pie.
2. The peanut butter is _____ .
3. The bread is _____ , too.
4. The chocolate cake is the _____ of all the cakes.
5. Orange juice is _____ than grape juice.
6. The toasted marshmallows are _____ than the untoasted ones.
7. The pecan muffins are the _____ of all four kinds here.
8. The bananas are _____ .
9. Peaches are _____ than the bananas.
10. Tangerines are the _____ fruit in the world.

Read the sentences again. This time add *bad, worse,* or *worst* to each one. Write them on your paper.

8 Recognizing Adverbs

To Read and Think Over

You know that adjectives are used to describe someone or something. *The big old house* gives you a more complete picture than the words *the house*. **Adverbs** do the same thing for verbs. Read this sentence.

Jane ran.

What words could you add to make the meaning more clear? Here are some ideas.

Jane ran **yesterday.**
Jane ran **here.**
Jane ran **quickly.**

Words like *yesterday, here,* and *quickly* are adverbs. Adverbs tell **how, where,** or **when.**

 ● On your activity paper write the answers to these questions.

1. Which adverb tells **how** Jane ran?
2. Which adverb tells **when** Jane ran?

3. Which adverb tells **where** Jane ran?

Talking Together

A. Discuss the answers you wrote on your activity paper.

B. Think of an adverb for each of these sentences. Discuss the sentences with your classmates.

    1. I will do my homework _____.
    2. I climbed the tree _____.
    3. We walked _____ to school.
    4. The bird chirps _____.
    5. Drive _____ on this road.

Use this Guideline to recognize adverbs.

A word is an adverb when it is used to tell <u>how</u>, <u>when</u>, or <u>where</u>.

To Do By Yourself

A. Each of these sentences has one adverb. Write the adverb on your paper.

1. We can get to school easily.
2. All we have to do is leave soon.
3. Florence has been here.
4. She looked up at the plane.
5. We climbed down.
6. She gets to work early.
7. She was late yesterday.
8. He walked calmly by the dog.
9. We ran fast.
10. It started to rain suddenly.

B. Use each of these words in a sentence. Write the sentences on your paper.

    around   suddenly   swiftly
    easily   quickly   soon
    boldly   usually   later

9 Using What You Have Learned

A. Read each sentence. Decide which form of the adjective in parentheses bests fits the sentence. Write each sentence on your paper. Review the GUIDELINES on page 261.

1. Have you ever done a job (hard) _____ than this job?
2. This is the (hard) _____ thing I have ever tried to do.
3. That rock is so (heavy) _____.
4. You'll need (strong) _____ muscles than those to lift it.
5. We'd be (happy) _____ to have some help.
6. Jason is the (good) _____ worker in the group.
7. Moving the rock was an (easy) _____ job than we thought.
8. It was the (bad) _____ job I had ever done.
9. Paula had a (good) _____ idea.
10. It should make us all feel (happy) _____ than we were.
11. This is a (good) _____ idea than Jason's.
12. Now we can move even the (large) _____ rocks in the garden.
13. Clearing the ground is (bad) _____ than weeding.
14. The ground is (rough) _____ now than it is in the spring.
15. Yes, January is the (cold) _____ month of the year.

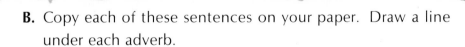

B. Copy each of these sentences on your paper. Draw a line under each adverb.

1. I gave a book review yesterday.
2. The crowd cheered noisily.
3. George finished work early.
4. We answered correctly.
5. I left the crowded room gladly.

267

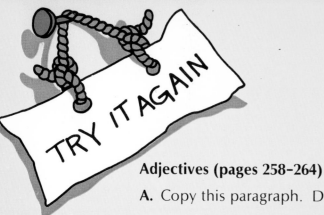

Adjectives (pages 258–264)

A. Copy this paragraph. Draw a line under each adjective.

We all watched the clever monkey. He was doing funny tricks. He rode on a tiny red bicycle. He pretended to be clumsy. He bumped into a tall, sad clown. The clown picked up the frisky monkey. Then the monkey pulled the clown's big shiny nose.

B. Copy these sentences. In each space write the correct form of the adjective in the parentheses.

(old)　　1. One of the _____ skyscrapers was the New York Tribune Building in Chicago.

(tall)　　2. The CN Tower in Toronto is the world's _____ free-standing structure.

(high)　　3. The Empire State Building used to be the _____ building in New York City.

(tall)　　4. It is _____ than the Chrysler Building.

(tall)　　5. Now, the towers of the World Trade Center are the _____ buildings in New York City.

(high)　　6. However, the Sears Tower in Chicago is _____ than the World Trade Center.

(long)　　7. This stick is _____ than that one.

(long)　　8. Use the _____ of all the sticks to toast the marsh-mallow.

(loud)　　9. The horn on your bike is _____ than mine.

(loud)　10. It is the _____ horn in the neighborhood.

C. Copy these sentences. Add the correct form of the adjective in parentheses.

(good)   1. My brother is the _____ batter on the baseball team.

(good)   2. Mike is also a _____ catcher.

(good)   3. He is a _____ catcher than Tom.

(bad)   4. Yesterday the team had a _____ day.

(bad)   5. It was the _____ game they ever played.

(bad)   6. It was _____ than the game they played last week.

(good)   7. I read a _____ ghost story.

(good)   8. It was the _____ ghost story I have ever read.

(bad)   9. What is the _____ thing you ever ate?

(bad) 10. Was it as _____ as yesterday's lunch?

Adverbs (pages 265–266)

Copy these sentences. Draw a line under each adverb.

1. Tom finished his work cheerfully.
2. Today he was going to the circus.
3. He walked quickly to the bus stop.
4. The bus arrived immediately.
5. Tom sat patiently on the bus.
6. Soon the bus arrived at the fairgrounds.
7. Tom walked excitedly to the entrance.
8. Then he bought a ticket.
9. He walked hurriedly to the main tent.
10. The people cheered loudly when the show began.

DO YOU REMEMBER ?

Sentence Pattern 1 (page 169)

Copy each sentence on your paper. Write *N* above each noun and *V* above each verb.

1. The circus came.
2. The lions are roaring.
3. Clowns are dancing.
4. A monkey chatters.
5. People cheer.

Combining Ideas (pages 200–201)

Copy this paragraph on your paper. Combine short sentences to make longer, more interesting ones.

I belong to a baseball team. It is called the Hawks. Last week we played a very important game. We were playing for the league championship. The other team was called the Falcons. Everyone thought that the Falcons would win. We were not going to let them, though. At first, the Falcons were ahead. Then we tied the game. Soon we were behind again. One of our team members hit a home run. He brought in two more runs. To everyone's surprise, the Hawks did win the game. The Hawks won the championship.

Using Commas, Quotation Marks, and Capital Letters (pages 185–187)

Write this letter correctly. Add commas, quotation marks, and capital letters where they are needed.

3301 taylor street
oakdale louisiana 71463
april 29 19__

dear rufus

I can hardly wait to tell you about the funny remark someone made to me yesterday. I had walked into Mr. Souza's watch and clock shop. Mr. Souza was behind the counter. my father sent me here with his watch because it is losing time I said. I asked can you fix it?

Yes I can take care of that replied Mr. Souza. Then he asked would you like to earn a dollar?

I said yes I would like to, Mr. Souza.

Mr. Souza said take this clock and deliver it to Mrs. Wilson on Maple Street. I lifted the clock. It was not very heavy, but it was hard to carry. I'll open the door for you said Mr. Souza.

You will never guess what happened next. I walked down the street with the clock. As i went by one woman, i knocked one of her packages out of her hand. I said I would pick it up for you, but my hands are full.

i can see that said the woman.

You'll never believe what she said next. She looked at the clock and said I should think it would be much easier for you to wear a wrist watch.

I don't think I'll ever forget that remark.

your friend
alan

On Your Own

1. You woke up this morning and found you were super strong. What will you be able to do with all your strength? What things will you fix? What things will you break? What strange things can happen to you? Write a story telling about your adventures.

2. Write a story telling what you would do if all of a sudden you became one of these things.

   ten feet tall
   invisible
   ten inches tall

3. Sometimes just a few words can give you an idea for a story or description. Take the words *an old clock*. Think about an old clock. How old is it? Does it hang on a wall or sit on a shelf? Did you find it in an attic or a junk shop? Try using your imagination with one of these groups of words. Write a story or a description about the words you choose.

   a lost puppy
   an old trunk
   a narrow, winding road

272

4. Pretend you've just won first prize in a contest. Your prize is an all-expense-paid trip to any place. Write a paragraph telling where you would like to visit. Describe what you will see and do.

BUSINESS LETTERS

Business letters are often written to places rather than to one person whom you know. They usually have only one idea. When you write a business letter, you are entering the busy world of business.

9

1 Business Letters

To Read and Think Over

Melissa wrote this letter to ask for free stamps. The kind of letter she wrote is called a **business letter.** Can you tell why Melissa wrote a business letter instead of a friendly letter?

383 Mountain Road
Cedar Grove, New Jersey 07009
December 7, 19___

Monster Mates
2822 Broadway
New York, New York 10024

Dear Monster Mates:

Please send me at the above address one sheet of the free Monster Stamps you advertised in the November issue of Kids Together magazine. I enclose twenty-five cents for postage and handling. Thank-you.

Sincerely yours,
Melissa Perkins

 ● Write the answer to each question on your activity paper.

1. Why did Melissa write to Monster Mates?

2. What did Melissa enclose with her letter?

3. To what address did Melissa ask Monster Mates to send the stamps?

Talking Together

A. Discuss with your classmates the answers you wrote on your activity paper.

B. Did Melissa's letter say exactly what she wanted? Did she need to add any more information? Why or why not?

C. What is the purpose of Melissa's business letter? How is it different from a friendly letter? Which kind of letter should be shorter? Why?

D. What are some other reasons for writing a business letter to a company or government office?

Follow these Guidelines when you write a business letter.

1. **At the beginning of your letter explain exactly what you want.**
2. **Say each thing only once. Make your letter as short as possible.**
3. **Don't say any more than the other person needs to know.**

To Do By Yourself

This business letter is too long. Rewrite it according to the GUIDELINES for writing a business letter. Keep only the sentences that are needed. Read the model letter to help you.

My friend Jennifer and I were looking through magazines yesterday. We thought it would be fun to order your rainbow decals. We each want a package. Send them to the address given. Enclosed is $1.00 for the two packages of decals plus twenty-five cents for postage and handling. Please send me two packages of the rainbow decals advertised on page 15 of the February issue of <u>Decorations</u>.

2 The Parts of a Business Letter

To Read and Think Over

A business letter has six parts. Five of them are the same as the five parts of a friendly letter. Study this business letter. Notice the six parts on the left side of the page. Which part does not appear in a friendly letter?

Heading	907 Redmount Street Brandon, Manitoba R7A 2A9 October 20, 19__
Inside Address	Circulation Manager Nature Guide 2618 Garcia Drive Boulder, Colorado 80302
Greeting	Dear Circulation Manager:
Body of the Letter	On August 3, I sent $5.00 to you for a one-year subscription to Nature Guide. I still haven't received my first issue of the magazine. Could you please find out whether you ever received my order? I would also like to know when I will start receiving the magazine.
Closing Signature	Yours truly, Lu-Anne Washington

 ● Answer these questions on your activity paper.

1. What are the six parts of a business letter?

2. Which part of a business letter does not appear in a friendly letter?

Talking Together

A. Discuss with your classmates the answers you wrote on your activity paper.

B. What is the purpose of the inside address?

C. How is the greeting in a business letter different from the greeting in a friendly letter? What punctuation mark is used after the greeting in a business letter?

Follow these Guidelines when you write a business letter.

1. Place the inside address before the greeting on the left side of the paper. The inside address tells the name or the title and address of the person or company to whom you are writing.
2. Use a colon (:) after the greeting in a business letter.

To Do By Yourself

Copy this letter on a sheet of paper. Add the heading, inside address, greeting, closing, and signature. Use your own name and address. The letter is being sent to the Public Relations Department, WBGL-TV, 120 Western Avenue, Allston, Massachusetts 02134.

May we please arrange to have someone from your station speak on careers in television? A group of thirty-five students in grades 4 through 8 is interested in this subject. We would like a speaker for a Tuesday or Thursday afternoon during the month of April. Thank you.

3 The Language of a Business Letter

To Read and Think Over

Read this letter. Pay special attention to the greeting, closing, and signature. How are they different from the greeting, closing, and signature of a friendly letter?

678 Brooks Highway
Moncton, New Brunswick
E1A   3E9
July 14, 19___

Trailside Camping Company
301 Cumberland Avenue
Portland, Maine 04102

Dear Trailside Camping Company:

   On June 15, I ordered the medium-size backpack frame on page 23 of your spring catalog. The frame arrived on July 12, but it is too big for me. I would like to exchange it for the small-size frame. I have sent the medium-size frame back to you.

Yours truly,
Ingrid Nielsen

● Answer these questions on your activity paper.

   1. What punctuation mark follows the greeting?
   2. How did the letter-writer sign her name?

Talking Together

A. Discuss with your classmates the answers you wrote on your paper.

B. The greeting in the model letter is "Dear Trailside Camping Company." If you knew the name of the person to write to at this company, would it be better to address the letter directly to that person? Why?

C. Think of some closings you would use for a business letter. Would you use them for a friendly letter? Why or why not? What are some closings you would not use in a business letter?

Follow these Guidelines when you write a business letter.

1. Use a person's name, a person's title, or the name of the company in the greeting. Use a colon after the greeting.
2. Use these closings in a business letter:
   Sincerely yours,   Yours truly,
   Begin the first word with a capital letter, and remember to use a comma after the closing.
3. Always sign your full name in a business letter.
   Dolores Potts   Louis A. Klein

To Do By Yourself

Read each of these inside addresses for a business letter. Write the greeting for each one correctly.

Credit Manager
Mott's Department Store
9802 Euclid Street
Akron, Ohio 44305

Mr. Donald McGrory
Assistant Superintendent
Gallup Public Schools
418 Loma Boulevard
Gallup, New Mexico 87328

Fortune House
8816 Ward Street
Storrs, Connecticut 06268

Ms. Isabel Rivera
Tourist Bureau
508 Pensacola Avenue
Orlando, Florida 32804

4 Filling Out Order Forms

To Read and Think Over

When you want to order something by mail, you can write a business letter or fill out an **order form.**

Study this order form. What can you order from it? What information is asked for in the form?

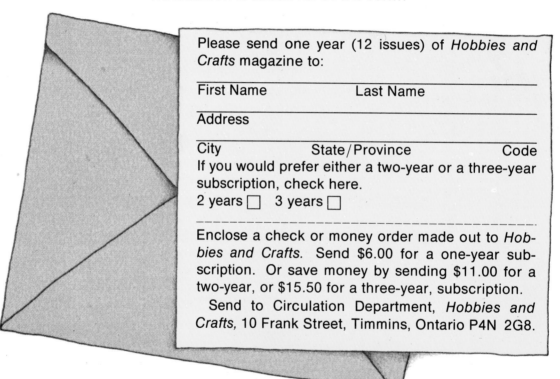

Please send one year (12 issues) of *Hobbies and Crafts* magazine to:

First Name   Last Name

Address

City   State/Province   Code

If you would prefer either a two-year or a three-year subscription, check here.

2 years ☐   3 years ☐

Enclose a check or money order made out to *Hobbies and Crafts.* Send $6.00 for a one-year subscription. Or save money by sending $11.00 for a two-year, or $15.50 for a three-year, subscription.

Send to Circulation Department, *Hobbies and Crafts,* 10 Frank Street, Timmins, Ontario P4N 2G8.

 ● Copy the order form on your activity paper. Fill in all the information that is needed to order *Hobbies and Crafts.* Decide if you want a one-, two-, or three-year subscription. Then draw an envelope. Put your address and the address of the magazine on it correctly.

Talking Together

A. Discuss the information you wrote on the order form. If you decided to order a one-year subscription, how much money would you need to send? How much money would you need to send for a two- or a three-year subscription?

B. Advertisements in newspapers often have order forms. Can you think of other places where you would find order forms?

C. Suppose you wanted to order a jacket from a catalog. What information would you need to complete the order form?

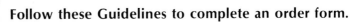

Follow these Guidelines to complete an order form.

1. Give all the information requested. Include choices of size and color, if needed.
2. Give your complete name and address, including your ZIP or postal code.
3. Always proofread an order form. Make sure you haven't left anything out or put anything in the wrong place. Check all numbers carefully.

To Do By Yourself

Read this ad. Then copy the order form. Fill in all the information needed to order a sweatshirt for yourself. Be sure to
proofread your work.

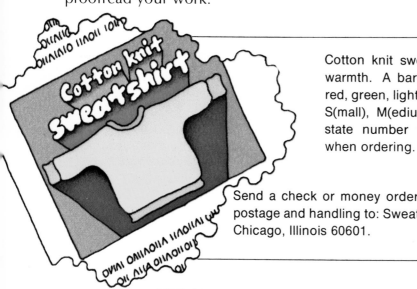

Cotton knit sweatshirt. Fleece-lined for warmth. A bargain at $4.98! Comes in red, green, light blue, or navy blue. Sizes S(mall), M(edium), and L(arge). Please state number wanted, color, and size when ordering.

Send a check or money order, including fifty cents for postage and handling to: Sweatshirts Unlimited, Box 503, Chicago, Illinois 60601.

ORDER FORM

Name_____

Address_____

City_____ State _____ ZIP _____

How Many	Name of Item	Style	Color	Size	Price
			Postage		.50
			Total Price		

5 Using What You Have Learned

A. How well do you write a business letter?

Write a business letter to order a deck of Magic Cards. You saw the cards advertised on television station RNK. Write to The Magic Shop at 1487 Second Avenue, New York, New York 10018. Be sure to include all the parts of a business letter in their correct order. Review the GUIDELINES on pages 277, 279, and 281.

B. How well do you fill out an order form?

Copy this order form on your paper. Fill in all the information you need to order two 18″ × 20″ Western Adventure wall posters at $1.50 each and one 20″ × 24″ Seascape poster at $2.00.

Send to:			
Name_____			
Address_____			
City _____ State _____ ZIP _____			

How Many	Name of Item	Size	Price
	Western Adventure wall poster		
	Seascape wall poster		
	Forest Scene wall poster		
		Postage	.50
		Total Price	

WORDS ARE INTERESTING

Prefixes and Suffixes

Study the labels under the pictures. Which are the base words? What word parts come *before* a base word? What word part comes *after* a base word?

usual   unusual

fear   fearless

spell   misspell

Word parts that come before a base word are called *prefixes.*

> **un-**, which means **not** or **opposite of.**
> **mis-**, which means **badly** or **wrongly.**

286

Word parts that come after a base word are called **suffixes.**

-ful, which means **full of** or **enough to fill.**
-less, which means **without.**

When you add prefixes or suffixes to a base word, you can often express your ideas in a shorter and more exact way.

Copy this story. When you come to a word group in bold-face type, look at the words in the word list. Find one word that can take the place of the word group. Use that word in the story.

The Case of the Missing Gerbil

"This classroom is still **not very neat,**" said Ms. Teachright. "That's why Teresa's gerbil may be **in the wrong place.**"

"It's **no use,**" sighed Teresa **without happiness.** "I feel there's nothing I can do about finding my **very lovely** little gerbil."

"Wait a minute," said Ms. Teachright **in a happy way.** "There is your gerbil!"

Everyone looked up. The gerbil was asleep in the corner.

"Just the right touch for a messy room," said Amos **with a great deal of thought.**

Word List

thoughtfully	misplaced	unpleasant	untidy
joylessly	joyfully	hopeless	beautiful

6 Writing a Paragraph

To Read and Think Over

A **paragraph** is a group of sentences that tell about only one thing. That one thing is called the **topic** of the paragraph. In a good paragraph, each sentence tells something new about the topic, and the sentences are in an order that makes sense.

Read the next paragraph. What is the topic? Do all the sentences belong in the paragraph? Are they in an order that makes sense? The sentences are numbered to make it easier to talk about them.

1. My favorite place to go after school is the new playground near our building. **2.** This is the place I like to go after school. **3.** The wall is hollow, and you can crawl through it as if it were a tunnel. **4.** It has a low wall all around the edge. **5.** Inside the playground there are wooden poles and towers to climb. **6.** You can get down from some of them by sliding down a slide. **7.** Some of them have ropes you can slide down. **8.** You can slide down either a slide or a rope. **9.** The ground is covered with sand so that you can jump down easily.

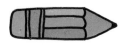 ● Write the answers to these questions on your activity paper.

1. Which of these three titles tells what the topic of the paragraph is?
   What I Like to Do After School
   The New Playground
   Why I Like Playgrounds

2. Which sentence is not in an order that makes sense?

3. Which two sentences repeat something that has already been told about the topic?

Talking Together

Discuss your answers with your classmates. If your teacher asks you, read the paragraph aloud. Take out the sentences that don't belong. Be sure all the sentences that remain are in an order that makes sense.

> **Follow these Guidelines to write a paragraph.**
> 1. **Make sure you know what the topic of the paragraph is.**
> 2. **Make sure each sentence tells something new about the topic.**
> 3. **Make sure the sentences are in an order that makes sense.**

To Do By Yourself

Rewrite this paragraph. Leave out any sentences that do not belong. Be sure the sentences are in an order that makes sense. Proofread your paper, and copy it over if you need to.

When my sister and I woke up yesterday, we had a surprise. It had snowed during the night. There was so much snow on the ground that school was closed for the day. We went outside without stopping for breakfast. There was no school that day. There were no footprints anywhere yet. All the trees and bushes were covered with snow. There was snow on everything. Our back steps had disappeared under a pile of snow. We use the back door so that we can leave our boots in the kitchen. We felt our way carefully down the steps. We felt like explorers on a strange planet. The snow came to the tops of our boots.

7 Beginning a New Paragraph

To Read and Think Over

When you write a paragraph, you write sentences that tell about one topic. Each time you begin to write about a new topic, you need to start a new paragraph.

Read these paragraphs that Susan wrote. What is the topic of the first paragraph? What is the topic of the second paragraph? Did Susan begin a new paragraph when she changed her topic?

When people think of sharks, they usually think of one kind of shark first. This is the large, greatly feared shark called the Great White Shark. It can be as long as 6.4 meters. Its underside is white, but its back is a grayish color. Its teeth are large and sharp with jagged edges.

Another kind of shark people often think about is the Basking Shark. It is one of the largest of all sharks. It can be as long as 13.7 meters. The Basking Shark has many small teeth. It eats small fish and plants.

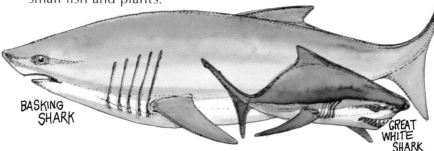

BASKING SHARK

GREAT WHITE SHARK

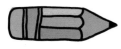 ● On your activity paper write the answers to these questions.

    1. What is the topic of Susan's first paragraph?
    2. What is the topic of Susan's second paragraph?
    3. Why did Susan start a new paragraph?

Talking Together

A. Discuss your answers with your classmates.

B. If Susan added a description of a Frilled Shark to her report, would she need to begin a new paragraph? Why?

Follow these Guidelines when you write more than one paragraph.

1. Begin a new paragraph each time you begin to write about a new topic.
2. Indent the first word of each paragraph.

To Do By Yourself

Read each paragraph. Then choose one of the sentences in the box as the topic sentence for each paragraph. Copy each paragraph on your paper. Begin each paragraph with the correct topic sentence.

A beetle's jaws are very large and powerful. A beetle has two pairs of wings. The outer pair of wings is heavy. The inner pair of wings is used for flying.

There are more kinds of beetles than there are of any other insect. Some kinds of beetles are smaller than a grain of salt. Other kinds of beetles are several inches wide.

There are more than 250,000 kinds of beetles in the world.

There are several ways to describe a beetle.

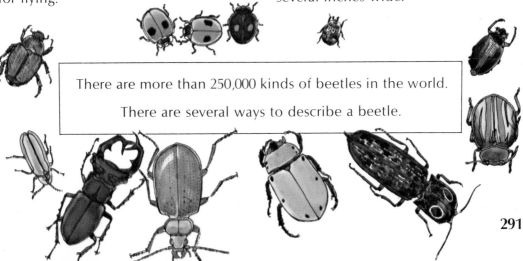

8 Writing Contractions

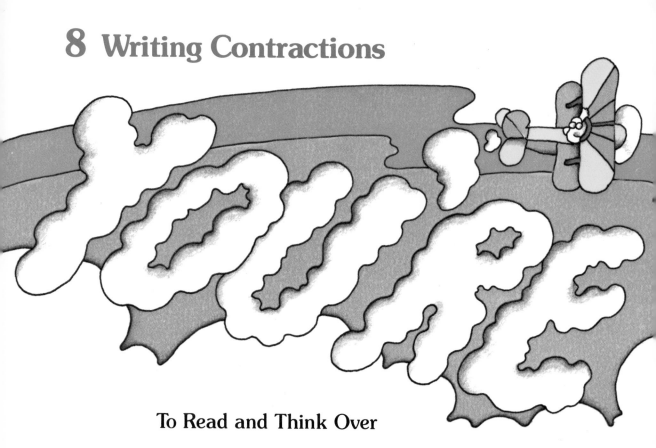

To Read and Think Over

The words **you** and **are** can be put together to make the contraction **you're.** In forming the **contraction,** the letter **a** was left out and an **apostrophe** (') put in its place.

Study these contractions and the words they stand for. Which letters are left out in each contraction?

isn't	=	is	+	not	I'm	=	I	+ am
aren't	=	are	+	not	you're	=	you	+ are
wasn't	=	was	+	not	he's	=	he	+ is
weren't	=	were	+	not	she's	=	she	+ is
don't	=	do	+	not	it's	=	it	+ is
doesn't	=	does	+	not	you'll	=	you	+ will
couldn't	=	could	+	not	we'll	=	we	+ will
hasn't	=	has	+	not	I've	=	I	+ have
won't	=	will	+	not	it's	=	it	+ has
can't	=	can	+	not	you'd	=	you	+ would

 ● Number your activity paper from 1 to 12. Copy the words beside the numerals. Then write the contraction that is formed from putting the words together.

1. do not
2. was not
3. she is

4. we will
5. I have
6. are not

7. cannot
8. he is
9. could not

10. you will
11. does not
12. will not

Talking Together

A. Discuss the contractions you wrote. What letters were left out of each contraction? Was more than one letter left out in some contractions?

B. Which contractions were formed by putting together a verb and the word *not?* Which contractions were formed by putting together a pronoun and a verb?

C. With your classmates, make up sentences using each contraction on your activity paper.

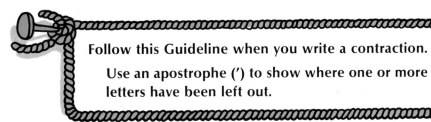

Follow this Guideline when you write a contraction.

Use an apostrophe (') to show where one or more letters have been left out.

To Do By Yourself

Rewrite this paragraph. Use a contraction in place of each pair of underlined words.

It has been snowing for days. But it is not very cold. It is a sunny day, so nice that you are not going to want to go indoors right away. I have been skating every day. Today I am going to take my sled out instead. You will have to join us one day. The park and the hill are good places to go sledding. They are both nearby, too. You would have a great time. We will go together soon.

9 Using Isn't, Aren't; Wasn't, Weren't; Doesn't, Don't

To Read and Think Over

The contractions **isn't, aren't, wasn't, weren't, doesn't,** and **don't** are used correctly in these sentences.

She **isn't** singing.	The kittens **aren't** playing.
Mark **wasn't** skating.	You **weren't** looking.
It **doesn't** make sense.	They **don't** stock it.
He **isn't** going.	You **don't** know.

Did you notice that *isn't, wasn't,* and *doesn't* are used when the subject is *he, she, it,* or a singular noun? When the subject of the sentence is *we, you, they,* or a plural noun, *aren't, weren't,* and *don't* are used.

 ● Number your activity paper from 1 to 6. Next to each numeral write the contraction that fits the sentence.

1. (Isn't, Aren't) this the day of the picnic?
2. (Doesn't, Don't) you want to pack a lunch?
3. It (doesn't, don't) have to be fancy.
4. We (wasn't, weren't) going to bring dessert.
5. (Wasn't, Weren't) Henry going to bring that?
6. (Isn't, Aren't) you glad we're going?

Talking Together

A. Discuss your answers with your classmates.

B. Practice these sentences aloud. Use the correct form.

isn't or aren't

Molly _____ here.   You _____ late.
We _____ sure.   It _____ cold.

wasn't or weren't

They _____ ready.   I _____ prepared.
He _____ tired.   It _____ dark.

doesn't or don't

The experts _____ know.   You _____ understand.
Alex _____ care.   She _____ sing.

Follow these Guidelines when you use contractions.

1. Use the contractions <u>isn't</u>, <u>wasn't</u>, or <u>doesn't</u> when the subject is <u>he</u>, <u>she</u>, <u>it</u>, or a singular noun.
2. Use the contractions <u>aren't</u>, <u>weren't</u>, or <u>don't</u> when the subject is <u>we</u>, <u>you</u>, <u>they</u>, or a plural noun.

To Do By Yourself

Copy these sentences. In sentences 1 to 5, use *isn't* or *aren't*. In sentences 6 to 10, use *wasn't* or *weren't*. In sentences 11 to 15, use *doesn't* or *don't*.

1. Terence _____ angry anymore.
2. You _____ surprised.
3. His friends _____ waiting for him.
4. He _____ going yet.
5. It _____ time to leave.
6. The eggs _____ cooking.
7. The water _____ boiling.
8. The children _____ awake yet.
9. We _____ hungry.
10. Breakfast _____ ready.
11. Harriet _____ understand.
12. That machine _____ work.
13. The owners _____ care.
14. They _____ have any change.
15. I _____ want an ice-cream cone.

10 Using "Not" Words

NEVER

NONE

"Don't use two when you need only one."

To Read and Think Over

Many words have the meaning of "not." You know that contractions that end in *n't* have this meaning. Study this chart of other words that have the meaning of "not."

> Never means "not ever."
> Nothing means "not anything."
> None means "not any."
> Nobody means "not anybody."

These sentences show different ways of saying "not" correctly. What word in each sentence has the meaning of "not"?

1. Roland never eats too much.
2. Shana has nothing to say.
3. Joseph has nothing to do.
4. Nobody wanted to play baseball today.
5. Grace has none.

Notice that only one "not" word is used in each sentence.

 ● Number your activity paper from 1 to 5. Beside the numeral write the "not" word that is used in the sentence with the same numeral.

Talking Together

A. Discuss your answers with your classmates. Do you understand what a "not" word is? If you do not, ask your teacher to explain it.

B. Which of these words are "not" words? Use each "not" word in a sentence.

no	some	was	wasn't
anywhere	nowhere	didn't	did
no more	anymore	isn't	is

C. Close your books and listen while your teacher reads this story. Listen to the "no" or "not" words used correctly.

Peter wanted to surprise his family. He decided to begin making dinner. He looked in the refrigerator. There weren't __1__ (any, no) eggs. There __2__ (was, wasn't) no milk either. There were __3__ (any, no) vegetables. He couldn't find __4__ (anything, nothing) __5__ (anywhere, nowhere). There wasn't __6__ (any, none) flour or sugar. There was __7__ (anything, nothing) to fix for dinner. He hadn't __8__ (ever, never) seen that before. Peter didn't have __9__ (any, no) idea of what to do. Just then he saw a note and a shopping list on the kitchen table. They were from his mother. "Dear Peter," it said, "there __10__ (is, isn't) no food in the house. When I get home, we'll go to the store."

Follow this Guideline when you use <u>not</u> words.

Do not use two <u>no</u> or <u>not</u> words when you need only one.

To Do By Yourself

Write the story on your paper. Choose the correct word from those in parentheses.

11 Using What You Have Learned

A. How well do you write paragraphs?

Write two short paragraphs of three sentences each, describing an animal or a place. Remember to begin a new paragraph when you change the topic. Proofread your work.

B. How well do you form contractions?

In each sentence, write the correct contraction for each pair of underlined words.

1. <u>She is</u> a good thinker.
2. <u>I am</u> sure he can answer your question.
3. <u>He is</u> always willing to help.
4. <u>You are</u> next in line.
5. <u>We will</u> meet later.

C. How well do you use contractions?

Write these sentences. Use the correct form of the contraction in parentheses.

1. Lena _____ (isn't, aren't) using that eraser.
2. Danny _____ (doesn't, don't) want to borrow it.
3. The papers _____ (wasn't, weren't) hung on the bulletin board.
4. We _____ (doesn't, don't) know where they are.

D. How well do you use "not" words?

Write these sentences on your paper. Choose the correct word in parentheses.

1. Lou didn't find (anything, nothing).
2. There weren't (any, no) clues at all.
3. He had (never, ever) seen anything so mysterious.
4. There wasn't (anyone, no one) to ask about it.
5. There was (anywhere, nowhere) else to look.

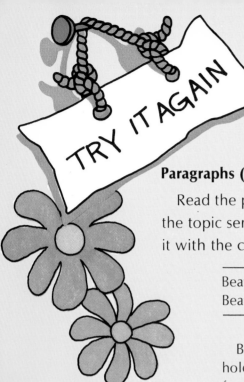

TRY IT AGAIN

Paragraphs (pages 288–289)

Read the paragraph. Then decide which of the sentences is the topic sentence. Copy the paragraph on your paper. Begin it with the correct topic sentence.

Beaver fur has been considered valuable for over 300 years. Beavers are very useful in flood control.

Beavers build dams across small streams. These dams hold back water in a wet season. They also keep streams from flowing too rapidly. The dams cut down the amount of water that flows from small streams into larger ones. This helps to prevent flooding by rivers.

Contractions (pages 292–295)

A. Copy each sentence. Write the correct contraction for each underlined word or words.

1. She <u>could not</u> find her homework paper.
2. She <u>cannot</u> go to afternoon gym.
3. Her friends <u>do not</u> want to go without her.
4. She <u>does not</u> want them to wait for her.
5. They said that <u>they will</u> wait in the library.

B. Write these sentences. Use the correct form of the contraction in parentheses.

1. Peter (isn't, aren't) home today.
2. His friends (doesn't, don't) know where he is.
3. Yesterday he (wasn't, weren't) at the playground.
4. Danny (isn't, aren't) home, either.
5. Maybe they (isn't, aren't) planning to come to the game.
6. This book (doesn't, don't) belong to me.
7. There (doesn't, don't) seem to be a copy in the library.
8. (Doesn't, Don't) you agree that it's a good story?
9. The story (wasn't, weren't) a cowboy story.
10. (Wasn't, Weren't) you planning to give a review about that story?

No and Not Words (pages 296–298)

Write these sentences. Use the correct word from the words in parentheses.

1. Hasn't (nobody, anybody) telephoned me, Sue?
2. There haven't been (no, any) calls today.
3. Won't Mary (never, ever) call?
4. She said she had (nothing, anything) to do this morning.
5. She wasn't planning to go (anywhere, nowhere).
6. There were (no, any) lights during the storm.
7. We had (any, no) candles.
8. There weren't (no, any) in the house.
9. No one (could, couldn't) find a flashlight.
10. There wasn't (anybody, nobody) home upstairs.

Recognizing Adjectives (pages 258–259)

Copy this paragraph. There are ten adjectives. Circle each one.

Today was an exciting day. A new circus had come to town. An enormous elephant walked in the parade. White horses pranced across the ring. A sad-looking clown drove a tiny car. A daring acrobat walked on a high rope without a net. A fierce tiger jumped through a flaming hoop.

Using Correct Word Forms (pages 260–264)

Copy these sentences, using the correct form of the adjective in parentheses.

(cold)   1. Today is a very _____ day. Tomorrow may be _____ than today. Last week we had the _____ day of the year so far.

(young)   2. I have a very _____ sister. She is only two years old. She is _____ than my brother, who is five. She is the _____ child in our family.

(good)   3. Today our team was _____ than it usually is. Yesterday was not a _____ day at all. Pete is the _____ pitcher on our team and was sick.

(bad)   4. My lunch today was the _____ one I have ever eaten. It was even _____ than yesterday's lunch. I sure hope tomorrow's lunch won't be as _____.

302

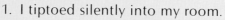

Recognizing Adverbs (pages 265–266)

Copy these sentences. Draw a line under each adverb.

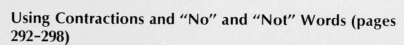

1. I tiptoed silently into my room.
2. I opened the box cautiously.
3. The package opened easily.
4. A little puppy looked at me eagerly.
5. I hugged him tightly.

Using Contractions and "No" and "Not" Words (pages 292–298)

Copy these sentences. Use the correct words in parentheses.

You (doesn't, don't) have any more cookies. (Wasn't, Weren't) you planning to go home when you finished eating? Jane and Beth (isn't, aren't) going home now. Beth (hasn't, haven't) finished her snack. She (doesn't, don't) usually go (nowhere, anywhere) with us. I'm glad she (wasn't, weren't) busy with (any, no) plans today.

On Your Own

1. You had saved your money and bought a new toy. The first time you used it, you found something wrong with it. Write a letter to the store or the company that made the toy. Tell them what happened to the toy.

HELP WANTED

WRITE: MS. C. A. ROSE, THE DAISY SHOP

2. On your way home from school you saw this sign in the flower shop window. You thought you would really like the job. Write a letter to Ms. C. A. Rose, applying for the job. Tell Ms. Rose why you think you would be good at the job.

3. You have read many books you have liked. Choose one of the books you have enjoyed the most. Write a letter to the author saying why you liked the story. If you wish, you might also suggest an idea for another story the author might write.

4. You and your classmates are planning a class picnic on Saturday. The class is trying to decide on a place to have the picnic. Where do you think it should be held? Think of several possible places. Think of reasons for and against each place. Then write a paragraph telling where you think the picnic should be held and why that place would be best.

YOUR
LANGUAGE
HANDBOOK

The Sentence

Definition

A sentence is a group of words that tells or asks something by itself. It starts with a capital letter and ends with a mark of punctuation.

Activity   Four of these word groups are sentences. Copy the sentences on your paper.

1. Dogs and cats.
2. The cat was in the tree.
3. The dogs barked.
4. Higher in the tree.
5. The dogs couldn't climb the tree.
6. The cat was safe.

Kinds of Sentences

A statement tells something. It ends with a period.

I ran to school.

A question asks something. It ends with a question mark.

Do you want some fudge?

A command asks or orders. It ends with a period.

Please pass the potatoes.

An exclamation shows surprise or strong feeling. It ends with an exclamation mark.

The movie was terrific!

Activity Copy these sentences. Add the correct punctuation. Show what kind of sentence each is by writing *S* for statement, *Q* for question, *C* for command, and *E* for exclamation next to each sentence.

1. Are you going to the store
2. Return these bottles for me
3. I will ride my bicycle
4. What a heavy load she carried

Subject and Predicate

The subject tells who or what is talked about in the sentence.

My dog ate the meat. Bob raked the yard.

The predicate tells something about the subject.

My dog wagged his tail. The cat meowed.

Activity Copy each sentence on your paper. Draw one line under the subject and two lines under the predicate.

1. José wrote a story.
2. The story was about a haunted house.
3. The class listened to the story.
4. They knew the house in the story.
5. The house belonged to an old sea captain.

Simple Subject and Simple Predicate

The simple subject is the main noun or pronoun in the subject.

The man bought an ice-cream cone.

The simple predicate is the verb in the predicate.

Bob ordered three scoops. I will try a banana split.

Activity   Copy each sentence. Draw one line under each simple subject and two lines under each simple predicate.

1. We walked to the park.
2. We will play soccer.
3. The basketball needs some air.
4. Randy owns an air pump.
5. He will fix the basketball.

Parts of Speech

Nouns

A word is a noun when it is used to name a person, place, or thing.

The book is about spiders and snakes.

A noun is often preceded by a **determiner.** A determiner signals that a noun follows.

a day   this week   that book   the dog   those people

Activity

Copy each sentence. Circle each determiner. Underline each noun.

1. This book is fascinating.
2. A friend gave it to me.
3. It is about a hidden treasure.
4. This treasure was found by some children.
5. Those children had an exciting adventure.

Common and Proper Nouns

A word is a proper noun when it is used to name a particular person, place, or thing. A proper noun always begins with a capital letter.

Scott went to Wilson School in April.
Next Tuesday Sheri will move to Elm Street.

All other nouns are common nouns.

The boy walked his dog in the park.

Activity Copy the word or word group beside each numeral. Then write *common noun* or *proper noun* after each one to tell which it is.

1. city
2. New York
3. summer
4. July
5. mountain
6. Fifth Avenue
7. baby
8. Wednesday
9. tree
10. Harvey

Singular and Plural Nouns

A word is a singular noun when it names one thing.

He took his **ball** and **bat** out of the **closet**.

A word is a plural noun when it names more than one thing.

We put away the **skis** and **boots**.

1. The plural of most nouns is formed by adding **s** to the singular.
       bicycle   bicycle**s**   apple   apple**s**

2. The plural of nouns that end in **ch, sh, s** or **x** is formed by adding **es.**
       punch   punch**es**   bush   bush**es**
       circus   circus**es**   fox   fox**es**

3. The plural of some nouns that end in **o** is formed by adding **s.** Some add **es.**
       piano   piano**s**   hero   hero**es**

4. The plural of many nouns that end in **y** is formed by changing **y** to **i** and adding **es.** Some add only **s.**
       party   part**ies**   baby   bab**ies**   tray   tray**s**

5. The plural of nouns that end in **f** or **fe** is formed by changing the **f** to **v** and adding **es.**
       calf   cal**ves**   life   li**ves**

Activity   Write the plural form of the noun in each group of words.

1. the last day
2. the sour tomato
3. the howling wolf
4. the white bridge
5. the colored candy
6. the wooden box
7. the flat board
8. the long brush
9. the tall church
10. the best guess

Possessive Nouns

A word is a possessive noun when it shows possession or ownership.

my **friend's** book
the book **that belongs to my friend**

his brother's whistle
the whistle **that belongs to his brother**

1. Add an apostrophe and **s** to a singular noun.
     the boss's desk   the book's title

2. Add just an apostrophe to a plural noun that ends in **s.**

     the ships' harbor   the boys' treehouse

3. Add an apostrophe and **s** to a plural noun that does not end in **s.**
     the men's department   the people's park

Activity   Write the possessive form of each of these nouns.

1. men
2. boys
3. ladies
4. lady
5. books
6. apple
7. stone
8. brothers
9. children
10. engines

Pronouns

A word is a pronoun when it is used to take the place of a noun. A **personal pronoun** takes the place of a certain person, or thing, or group of people or things.

Dan and Al went to the movie. They watched it twice.

This chart shows the singular and plural forms of personal pronouns.

Singular	Plural
I, me	we, us
you	you
he, she, it	they
him, her	them

Activity

Copy these sentences on your paper. Use the correct personal pronoun in place of the underlined words.

1. Jan and Ed went to the beach.
2. Ms. Jones gave Jan and Ed a ride.
3. The car was quite old.
4. Ed heard a funny noise.
5. Ms. Jones looked at the engine.

Verbs

A word or group of words is a verb when it is used to show action.

Beth had washed the windows.

Activity   Copy these sentences. Underline each verb.

1. It rained today.
2. Then the clouds drifted away.
3. A rainbow appeared in the sky.
4. Lucy closed her umbrella.
5. Jack rushed outside.
6. He walked in the puddles.
7. The sun was shining.

Verb Tenses

Verbs change their form or tense to show a change in time.
Verbs that show what is happening now are in the **present
tense.**

I **cook** and **bake.**

Verbs that show what happened in the past are in the **past
tense.** Most verbs add the ending **ed** or **d** to show the past
tense.

I **cooked** and **baked.**

Activity   Change the time in each statement from present to past. Write
the new statements on your paper.

1. We plant a garden.
2. I use a shovel.
3. We water the soil.
4. I place seeds in the soil.
5. We fence the yard in.
6. We wait for the plants to grow.
7. We weed the garden.

The Special Verb <u>Be</u>

The verb <u>be</u> does not show action. It shows that something <u>is</u> or that something <u>exists</u>.

This book **is** interesting. Dan **is** a reader.

This chart shows the forms of **be** in the present and past tenses.

Present Tense	
I am here.	We are here.
You are here.	You are here.
He is here.	They are here.
She is here.	
It is here.	

Past Tense	
I was here.	We were here.
You were here.	You were here.
He was here.	They were here.
She was here.	
It was here.	

Activity Number your paper from 1 to 5. Copy these sentences. Write a correct form of the verb **be** in each space.

1. The sun _____ bright today.
2. We _____ at the park.
3. I _____ there yesterday.
4. The park _____ empty then.
5. Today many people _____ in the park.

Adjectives

A word is an adjective when it is used to describe something or someone.

The tall boy plays basketball.

Activity Copy these sentences. Underline each adjective.

1. It was a wonderful hike.
2. We climbed the steep mountain.
3. Blue wildflowers grew on the top.
4. A small stream ran down the side.
5. The bright sun shone overhead.

Adverbs

A word is an adverb when it is used to tell <u>how</u>, <u>when</u>, or <u>where</u>.

The girl walked slowly. Her leg throbbed painfully.

Activity Copy each of these sentences. Underline each adverb.

1. We are going hiking there.
2. Let's pack our gear soon.
3. Abe wants to leave immediately.
4. He quickly put his hiking shoes on.
5. Finally we are ready.

Usage

Adjectives and Adverbs

The word **good** is used to tell what kind of person, place, or thing is being described.

Sam is a good **tennis player.**

The word **well** is used to tell how something is done.

He **played** well in the state finals.

Activity   Copy these sentences, choosing *good* or *well.*

1. Did you have a (good, well) day in gym class?
2. I did (good, well) on the parallel bars.
3. I didn't do as (good, well) as Jimmy.
4. He is a (good, well) athlete.
5. Some day I will be as (good, well) as he is.

Comparing with Adjectives

The ending **er** can be added to many adjectives to compare two people or things.

Ted is **tall.**
Jake is **taller** than Ted.

The ending **est** can be added to many adjectives to compare more than two people or things.

It is **warm** today.
It is **warmer** than yesterday.
It is the **warmest** day this week.

Activity   Complete this chart by writing the **er** and **est** forms of each adjective.

One person or thing	Two people or things	More than two people or things
1. low	_____	_____
2. small	_____	_____
3. cold	_____	_____
4. quick	_____	_____
5. high	_____	_____

Use **better** or **worse** to compare two people or things.

John is better at baseball than George.
John is worse at basketball than George.

Use **best** or **worst** to compare more than two people or things.

Jill is the best batter on the team.
Ann is the worst catcher on the team.

Activity   Copy these sentences. Write *good, better,* or *best* in each space.

1. Roberta is a _____ athlete.
2. She is the _____ runner in our class.
3. She is a _____ jumper than Tonia.
4. Roberta is a _____ batter also.
5. But Cindy is a _____ batter than Roberta.

Copy these sentences. Write *bad, worse,* or *worst* in each space.

1. This is the _____ dinner I have ever eaten.
2. It was even _____ than the burned spaghetti.
3. It was a _____ idea to boil the vegetables.
4. They taste _____ than before.
5. This is the _____ recipe in the book.

Negatives

Do not use two "no" or "not" words in a sentence when only one is needed.

We have **no** tomatoes in the garden.
There have**n't** been any for two weeks.

Activity Copy these sentences, using the correct word in parentheses. Remember to use only one "no" or "not" word if only one is needed.

1. Isn't there (anyone, no one) who knows how to put this thing together?
2. Nothing seems to fit (anywhere, nowhere).
3. Haven't you (any, no) time to help me?
4. I'll never start (a, no) project like this again.

Pronouns

When you speak of yourself and others, name yourself last.

Lee and I

When you speak of yourself and others, use **I** and **me** correctly. To make sure you have chosen the correct form, use **I** or **me** alone in the sentence.

Are you going to the store with Tony and me?

Yes, Gloria and I will be ready in a minute.

Activity Copy these sentences, using *I* or *me*.

1. Jan and _____ are going to the park.
2. Do you want to come with her and _____ ?
3. She and _____ like to play basketball there.
4. You and _____ used to be a good team.

Verb Forms That Agree with Subjects

When the subject is **he, she, it** or a singular noun, use the **s** form of a verb.

She runs.   **The** dog barks.   It tastes **good.**

When the subject is **I, we, you, they,** or a plural noun, never use the **s** form of a verb.

We run.   **The** dogs bark.   They taste **good.**

Activity   Copy these sentences, using the correct verb in parentheses.

1. My uncle (own, owns) a grocery store.
2. My brother and I (works, work) in the store.
3. Tom (sweep, sweeps) the floor every morning.
4. We (carry, carries) groceries for the people.
5. Mr. Baucus (shop, shops) at this store.

When the subject is **he, she, it,** or a singular noun, use these forms of the following verbs:

does, is, was, doesn't, isn't, wasn't

When the subject is **we, you, they** or a plural noun, use these forms of the following verbs:

do, are, were, don't, aren't, weren't

When the subject is **I,** use these forms of the following verbs:

do, am, was, don't, wasn't

Activity   Copy these sentences, using the correct verb in parentheses.

1. Jane (do, does) her homework in her room.
2. Her books (is, are) easy to find there.
3. She (was, were) a champion diver.
4. Jane (doesn't, don't) brag about it.
5. I know she (is, are) a better swimmer than I (am, are).

Using Correct Verb Forms

Use a helping word such as *has, have, had, is, are, was,* or *were* with these words: **eaten, come, done, given, run, seen,** and **gone.**

Never use a helping word with these words: **ate, came, did, gave, ran, saw,** and **went.**

Activity   Copy the sentences. Choose the correct word in parentheses.

1. We (ate, eaten) at Primo's Pizza Palace.
2. Have you ever (ate, eaten) one of Primo's specials?
3. Have you (came, come) to see John?
4. No, I (came, come) to see you.
5. Has she (did, done) well in the track meet?
6. She (did, done) very well in the high jump.
7. We (gave, given) a party for our teacher, Ms. Rogers.
8. She has been (gave, given) a job at another school.
9. I have never (ran, run) across this field before.
10. She (ran, run) across it last week.
11. The first robin of spring was (saw, seen) by the class today.
12. We (saw, seen) it in the tree by our window.
13. Bill has (went, gone) shopping.
14. He (went, gone) to the supermarket on the corner.

Words That Sound Alike

The word **their** means "belonging to" or "owned by" more than one person or animal.

The word **there** has a number of different meanings. Often it means "in" or "at that place."

The girls brought their sneakers.
They put them over there.

Activity   Copy these sentences, choosing *there* or *their*.

1. Are (there, their) any seats left on the bus?
2. (There, Their) is one seat in the back.
3. The twins have (there, their) books on it.
4. I'll sit (there, their).
5. Then I can ask them about (there, their) new canary.

The word **two** is a number. It has no other meaning.

The word **too** means "also" or "more than enough."

The word **to** has many different meanings.

I ate two peaches.
The third one was too ripe.
Mom went to the store to get some more.

Activity   Copy this paragraph, filling in the spaces with the correct word *to, too,* or *two.*

Gina and Andy went _____ an exhibit of Thomas Edison's inventions yesterday. The _____ of them saw over a hundred inventions. Some of them were the light bulb, the phonograph, and the microphone. They saw a motion picture that Edison made, _____. One of the guides showed them how _____ make a recording of their voices.

Capitalization and Punctuation

Apostrophes

Use an apostrophe in a contraction to show where one or more letters have been left out.

do not **don't**   was not **wasn't**   they are **they're**
is not **isn't**

Add an apostrophe and *s* to a singular noun to show owner-ship.

the child's toy

Use just an apostrophe with a plural noun that ends with *s* to show ownership

the ladies' briefcases

Add *s* and an apostrophe to a plural noun that does not end in *s* to show ownership

the men's jackets

Activity   Copy these sentences. Use the correct possessive form for each underlined word.

1. My <u>dogs</u> name is Sandy.
2. The <u>girls</u> mothers are showing movies.
3. The <u>boys</u> fathers are cooking hot dogs.
4. The <u>womens</u> coats are in the closet.
5. I bought the sandwich at <u>Sams</u> Shoppe.

Write five sentences using a contraction in each.

Capital Letters

Capital letters are used for the following kinds of words:

1. The first word of a sentence.
     The dog barked.

2. The name of a person.
     Steve, Francine

3. The words *Mr., Mrs., Ms.,* or *Miss.*
     Ms. ogers

4. The name of a pet.
     Jingles

5. Each important word in the name of a special place.
     Boston Public Library

6. Each important word in the name of a special day.
     New Year's Day

7. Each word in the name of a street.
     Fourth Street

8. Each word in the name of a city or town.
     Mexico City

9. Each word in the name of a state.
     Prince Edward Island

10. The first word in the greeting of a letter.
     Dear friend,

11. The first word in the closing of a letter.
     Yours truly,

12. The name of a month and day of a week.
     Tuesday   May

13. The word I.
     I will stay.

14. Each important word in a title.
     Treasure Island

Pretend that you have just spent a week some place that you have always wanted to visit. Now you are writing a friend about it. Fill in the spaces with things you saw and did on your trip. Be sure to use capital letters correctly.

(your address)
(today's date)

dear _____,

   i want to tell you about the fantastic trip i took when our class had a week off for (special day). _____ and i went to _____. we went by _____. some of the things we did were _____, _____, and _____. when we were there, we met _____, who was very nice. we were given a _____ to keep as a pet. i'm going to call mine _____. after we got back, our teacher, _____, asked us to write a report for the class. i hope that some day you will have a chance to go there.

                         your friend,

                         (your name)

Commas

Commas are used in the following ways:

1. To separate words or groups of words in a series. Use the word *and* or *or* between the last comma and the last word or group of words.

    Sally, Pete, and I   oranges, apples, or potatoes

2. After the word *yes* or *no* when it begins the answer to a question.

    Yes, I'll be there.   No, I won't forget.

3. Between the city or town and the state or province.

    Little Rock, Arkansas   Halifax, Nova Scotia

4. Between the day and the year in a date.
   July 1, 1867

5. After the greeting in a friendly letter.
   Dear Cherita,

6. After the closing in a letter.
   Sincerely,

Activity   Copy this letter on your paper, using commas where they are needed.

---

102 Sider Street
Stratford Connecticut
March 25 19__

Dear Uncle Fred

   Thank you for sending me the bat ball and catcher's mitt. Yes it was really forgetful of me to leave them at your house. My baseball game is this afternoon.

Yours truly
Ben

Period, Question Mark, and Exclamation Point

Use a **period** at the end of a statement.
Use a **period** at the end of a command.
Use a **period** after an initial or an abbreviation.
Use a **question mark** at the end of a question.
Use an **exclamation point** at the end of an exclamation.

What a huge watermelon!
Where did you get it?
I bought it at Mr. Tom C. Borden's market.
Please put it down.

Activity   Copy these sentences, adding correct punctuation.

1. Wow, what a surprise
2. What is it
3. It's an iguana
4. Mrs Ann R Michaels gave it to me
5. Please put it back into the box

Quotation Marks

Use **quotation marks** before the first word of a direct quotation. Put quotation marks after the last word and the final punctuation mark of the direct quotation.

"Are you coming to the party?" Ray asked.
"I'll be there at 8 o'clock," answered Jill.

Activity   Copy each of these direct quotations on your paper. Use quotation marks where they are needed.

1. What a beautiful day! exclaimed Marty.
2. Let's play soccer, suggested Tracy.
3. Do you have a soccer ball? asked Pete.
4. Bill has a soccer ball, said Francine.
5. I'll go and borrow it, Paul replied.

Index

CREDITS

Contributing Writer: Ellen D. Kolba
Design and Production: Kirchoff/Wohlberg, Inc.
Cover Illustration: Jan Pyk

Illustrators:
Marc Brown: 110–112, 114, 122, 126, 129, 131–135
Lynne Cherry: 12–13
Brian Cody: 210–211
Helen Cogancherry: 36–37, 44–45, 48, 54–57, 60–61, 64–65, 68–69, 78–79, 86, 97, 159, 160, 163, 165, 167, 169–171, 173, 214–215, 220–225, 228, 230–233, 235–237, 288–289
Arlene Dubanevich: 38–39, 70–73, 102–105, 138–141, 174–177, 206–209, 240–243, 268–271, 300–303
Frank Fretz: 18–19, 35, 148–149
Jennifer Kirchoff: 244–245
Justin Kirchoff: 244–245
Ron LeHew: 96
Erica Merkling: 40–41
Lyle Miller: 24–25, 58–59, 88–89, 194–195, 226–227, 286–287
Carol Nicklaus: 20–22, 26–34, 50, 82–84, 187–189, 254
Stella Ormai: 248–253, 255, 258, 262–265, 267
Judy Pelikan: 52, 219
Jan Pyk: 14–17, 46–47, 51, 63, 66–67, 80–81, 87, 90–92, 94, 99–101, 118–119, 124, 136, 146, 152–153, 156–157, 256–257, 277, 282, 284–285, 292, 294
Charles Robinson: 279, 280, 298
John Wallner: 182–185, 190–193, 198–199, 202–205, 260
Bari Weissman: 158, 161, 162, 164, 166, 172, 196–197, 200, 272–273, 296–297

Photographs:
10–11 Photo Researchers: 10 *t* Peter Buckley, *b* Larry Mulvehill, *r* Sherry Suris; 11 *t* Dick Rowan, *b* Hans Namath. **23** Ingbert Grüttner. **41–109** Photo Researchers: 41 *l* Ronny Jacques, *r* Susan Johns; 42 *l* Edward Latteau, *r* Vivienne; 43 *t* M. Durrance, *b* Michael Philip Manheim; 74 *t l* Doug Fulton, *t r* Fritz Henle, *b l* Michael Philip Manheim, *t r* Elinor Beckwith; 75 Van Bucher; 76 *t* Michael Philip Manheim, *b* Roger Tory Peterson; 77 *t* Fournier, *b* Jackie Curtis; 106 *t l* National Audubon Society/Harry Engels, *t r* Richard Nairin, *b* Ylla; 107 *l* Kinne/Reynolds, *r* Steve Allen; 108 *l* Philip Greenberg, *r* James W. Strongin; 109 *t* Ronny Jacques, *b* Guy Gillette. **113** Ingbert Grüttner. **121** Photo Researchers: Russ Kinne. **142** Photo Researchers: Diane Rawson. **143** Stock Boston: Peter Vandermark. **144** Photo Researchers: *l* Kent and Donna Dannen, *t* Michael Philip Manheim, Lewis T. Fineman. **145** Photo Researchers: *t* Robert Goldstein, *b* Porterfield Chickering. **155** Ingbert Grüttner. **178–181** Photo Researchers: 178 *t* Peter Buckley, *l* Bruce Roberts, *r* Michael Hayman; 179 *t* Fred Lyon, *b* Susan Johns; 180 Joe Munroe; 181 *t* Susan Johns. **181** Judy Poe/Boston. **212** Photo Researchers: Larry Mulvehill. **213** Stock Boston: *t* Frank Siteman. Photo Researchers: *t r* Bruce Roberts, *b* Raimondo Borea. **218** Photo Researchers: Tom Burnside. **244** Ingbert Grüttner. **246–274** Photo Researchers: 246 *l* Dan Sudia, *r* Lee E. Battaglia; *t* Ronny Jacques, *b* Larry Mulvehill; 273 *t l* Slim Aarons, *t r* David Halpern, *b l* George Laycock, *b r* John Henry Sullivan Jr.; 274 *t* Larry Mulvehill. **274** Magnum: Burk Uzzle. **275** Magnum: *t* Paul Fusco, *b* Charles Harbutt. Photo Researchers: Erika Stone. **283** Ingbert Grüttner. **304** Photo Researchers: Edward Lettau. **305** Judy Poe/Boston.